Application Generators Using Fourth-Generation Languages

Richard Watts

PUBLISHED BY NCC PUBLICATIONS

British Library Cataloguing in Publication Data

Watts, Richard A.
Application generators using fourth-generation languages.
1. Application generators (Computer science)
I. Title
005.1'3 QA76.76.A6

ISBN 0-85012-543-X

First published in 1987 by:

NCC Publications, The National Computing Centre Limited, Oxford Road, Manchester M1 7ED, England.

Typeset in 11pt Times Roman by Typeface Limited, Portland House, 103 Portland Street, Manchester M1 6DF; and printed by Hobbs the Printers of Southampton.

ISBN 0-85012-543-X

Acknowledgements

We would like to thank all those individuals and organisations who have helped in the research or commented on the draft, in particular: Kit Grindley, Ted Cluff and the other members of the Industry Working Party on 4th Generation Languages, set up by the Institute of Data Processing Management during 1985. The following people and organisations also deserve mention for their help and encouragement:

Alan Alcock	(Land Rover)
Alan Mayne	(Arthur Young)
Jim Toller	(CCTA)
Brian Whitcombe	(Jaguar)

We are grateful to the following groups who listened to our presentations and gave their reactions to the ideas presented:

BCS Northern Ireland
Data General User Group
Honeywell DPS6 User Group
IDPM North West

Thanks are also due to the Central Computer and Telecommunications Agency for permission to reproduce the Product Survey Questionnaire as Appendix 2.

The Centre also acknowledges with thanks the support of the Electronics and Avionics Research Board for the project on which this book is based.

Introduction

THE STRUCTURE OF THIS BOOK

Readers will find it helpful first to see what is to be found in this book. It is recommended that all readers look at Chapters 1 and 2 which consider the place of Application Generators in today's data processing environment. This makes it plain that for a successful implementation of application generators the organisation of the data processing environment can be as important as the choice of language.

The following chapter (Chapter 3) talks about the needs and experiences of those organisations that have used application generators. Next (Chapter 4) the features of application generators are explored in more detail: it is most vital for the potential user to state what he needs before being diverted by particular features which in the event he may not need at all.

Chapter 5, of practical use, describes a method for evaluating one application generator against another. It is based on work on 'measuring quality' carried out by the National Computing Centre and others during 1981-4 as part of the SDSS Project (Specification and Development of Software Systems), which was sponsored by the Commission of the European Community. Details of the output of this project can be obtained from the sources listed in the bibliography. The evaluation method has been used in many practical situations.

The final chapter looks at the effective use of application generators. This puts into perspective the changes which the introduction of an application generator can induce. The perfect solution has not yet emerged, but nevertheless it is clear that the use of productivity tools can solve many problems. One must also try to ensure that the initial surge of productivity is not merely a short-term effect: it must be sustained. This means that changes in attitude as well as language are needed.

The National Computing Centre has been working on research in this area for a number of years. R F Lobell carried out a product survey published in 1983 under the title *Application Program Generators*. R A Chard followed this with *Evaluating Program Generators for Micros* published during 1985. In a closely allied field, A Mayne and M B Wood wrote *Introducing Relational Database* which was published in 1983.

In 1986 the opening of the Software Tools Demonstration Centre at the National Computing Centre's Manchester offices has given another forum where productivity tools such as those discussed in this book can be seen and tried.

Contents

1 Application Generators

PURPOSE OF THIS BOOK

It is widely acknowledged that the traditional methods of producing computer systems are not always satisfactory: using such methods it takes a long time to produce systems which, even then, cannot easily accommodate changes in the users' requirements. Since there are now alternative ways of implementing effective systems, it is right that today's data processing department should be aware of the possibilities – how, for example, to use the tools which are now available, to see whether they offer a cost-effective alternative to the continuing use of such languages as COBOL, PL/1, BASIC and FORTRAN.

Many organisations are now finding that the use of application generators, a subset of the larger group of fourth-generation languages, can solve some of their problems. Indeed James Martin (Martin, 1985) has stated that the productivity of application development must increase by two orders of magnitude over the next ten years. This, he says, cannot happen if computers are still programmed with COBOL and PL/1. Even if one doubts such claims, it is certain that great improvements can be made.

This book shows ways in which organisations of all sizes can benefit from the use of these tools, and also discusses how to choose the right product.

The experiences on which this book is based are concerned mainly with application generators which run on mainframe and minicomputers. Even so, there are many parallels with the world of personal computers, especially now that some of the products from the 'big league' machines are becoming available in microcomputer versions. More of this convergence will be seen as personal computers become more powerful, containing more of the facilities previously found only on larger machines. Nevertheless, it is more appropriate to concentrate for the time being on the minis and mainframe machines. One reason for this is that the personal microcomputer scene is particularly volatile.

The present book is not intended as a product survey. Such surveys already exist but are very liable to become out-of-date in a changing world. However, people should learn how to choose and use the application generator software now available: the principles involved will not date so quickly.

Another danger of product surveys is that the reader may expect a 'best buy' recommendation, where in reality the right choice for an organisation will depend on factors not covered by the product survey. The approach described in this book should encourage each organisation to consider its own needs properly.

WHAT IS AN APPLICATION GENERATOR?

An application generator is a software tool used for the development and production of application systems. It allows the developer to produce complete data processing systems – which can range from the simple to the extremely complex – without the need to make use of COBOL or other procedural languages. It can do this because it contains what are in effect powerful pre-programmed routines which are invoked and linked together to form the required system.

The application generator will in general contain the following basic constituents:

- a method of defining the file or database structure. This will often include a data dictionary or directory and may also allow reference to other data dictionary products;
- means of defining how data will be input to the system. Most systems developed with application generators are on-line systems, though in some cases batch systems can also be built. The application generator controls screen handling and formatting, validation and error messages;

- ways to specify the program logic and the necessary updating of files;
- a report generator allowing the production of on-line displays and printed reports;
- a query language, at least where it is desirable to allow end-users to have access to data held on the files controlled by the system. Regular access will normally be by means of regular reports or pre-programmed displays, but the query language allows more flexible ad-hoc enquiries to be made.

These productivity tools are also referred to as:

- application program generators;
- system building tools;
- high-productivity, general-purpose programming languages;
- fourth-generation languages.

The term 'application program generator' has been used to describe software tools that generate source code in a high-level language such as COBOL. An application generator, unlike a program generator, can produce all the programs required for the application system using a common, compatible set of definitions.

'System building tools' and 'high-productivity, general-purpose programming languages' are other phrases which have been used to describe this sort of software tool, but are not widely employed.

The term 'fourth-generation language' is certainly widely used but covers a wider field than 'application generator', because it includes such tools as query languages and report generators (which only carry out *some* of the functions of an application generator) as well as spreadsheets and decision support software. It has not therefore been used here as the generic name for this sort of product, even though it is often used in this way.

The most significant advantages of application generators are as follows:

- they make it easier to complete systems quickly. Thus the backlog of systems required can be tackled and there are fewer worries about deadlines;

— they are easier to learn, allowing reduced investment in training. People become productive sooner. In particular, they do not need to learn as much about the computer's operating system and teleprocessing software;

— the resultant systems are easier to understand and therefore to maintain. This is especially valuable where the business situation makes rapid changes necessary;

— some application generators allow users to develop their own systems. This can facilitate better use of the organisation's data.

Application generators are one of a number of productivity tools now available to help the DP function within an organisation. If they happen to suit a particular organisation and can be introduced in a cost-effective manner, they should be used. Potential users, however, should be quite clear what sort of products are required. The organisation is strongly advised to analyse its needs (regarding productivity and development) before choosing a fourth-generation language for its own use (see Chapter 5). First it needs to know what is available and how other organisations have used the tools.

POWERFUL SOFTWARE TOOLS

An application generator is a powerful software tool which allows one, with much less programming than a traditional language such as COBOL, to design and implement systems. The generator has a basic framework within which the generated system must be developed. Thus some of the more repetitive programming has already been done. The application generator allows input with validation of data and carries out the processing and manipulation of that data, as well as all the associated screen handling, file and database handling and reporting.

It will normally include its own data dictionary or directory, which may or may not be comprehensive – it may be an active dictionary (which will control the details of fields and files that can be used) or passive (merely reflecting the state of the files at any one time). Some products are either closely linked with the software producer's own data dictionary or have built-in interfaces to another data dictionary product.

Similarly with file and database handling, a product may use one of the following:

- its own database;
- the computer manufacturer's file handling or database software;
- another proprietary database;
- a combination of the above to suit the particular organisation.

It is advantageous for an established data processing organisation to use a combination of software which suits existing applications – if there are to be any links between the old and the new. Application generators which use their own data handling routines can usually access data from other applications, using perhaps external files. The critical factor may be how often it is necessary for external routines and applications to access data from within the generator's files: this can be difficult with some products.

People sometimes talk about 'true 4GLs': but since there is no agreed definition of fourth-generation languages, it is not particularly helpful to think in these terms. It is more useful to state positively some of the characteristics which make some application generators more powerful than others. The following attributes have been found to be useful (see for example CCTA 1983):

- the ability to navigate between different screens, ie to choose on any screen what screen will be seen next. This enables 'black-box' application systems to be constructed, ie systems where the users will be quite unaware of the underlying software;

- the ability to carry out logical procedures, as a response to input data, file data or other variables;

- the ability to carry out development and then to execute the code written without a complete or extended compilation processs. This ability to carry out 'dynamic generation' of systems is one of the features which have been most welcomed by DP professionals who have been 'converted' to 4GLs. (This topic is further discussed in Chapter 4.)

All generators allow a great saving in the number of lines of code, or its equivalent, that need to be written. Built-in routines do not need to be written anew for each application, and there are powerful individual commands. Some of the greatest savings come from the 'report writer' area of the application generator. Here there is nothing that has not been available in report-writing packages for some time. The advantage is that now such facilities are combined with all the other features of the application generator, with a common interface to learn. This will be found to be more convenient than to have separate products to carry out the two different functions – report writing and application generation – especially where the same staff are employed on both activities.

Other features are discussed in more detail in Chapter 4. The reader should note particularly features that assist with data security (eg control over access to particular files and fields). Even if not present within the application generator, these features may be provided by the database software.

2 Application Generators in the DP Environment

THE DP ENVIRONMENT

It is important to consider application generators in the context of today's data processing environment. This will highlight changes which have taken place in the world of the DP Manager in recent years, especially the increased pressure for results from reduced staff resources and the demand for systems that respond to changes in the business needs of the organisation. There has been an increase in pressure on development staff – caused in part by the difficulty in obtaining people with the right experience, but also by a decrease in budgets as personnel costs increase relative to hardware costs. This has recently been seen in, for example, the NCC Members Survey and the Urwick/*Computing* Survey.

Many organisations have stated that their main reason for looking for a development aid such as an application generator has been the need to get more work out of the same number of staff (or even fewer). This can be a particular problem in areas such as London and the South-East where there is a very high turnover of staff.

Another factor has been the reduction in computer costs: many organisations have preferred to obtain more computer power at reduced rates than to make actual savings. This has meant that they are willing to tolerate decreases in operational efficiency in order to achieve the staff productivity that they want. Add to this the fact that the users of computer systems have become more sophisticated and demanding. The personal computer revolution encourages people to have control of their own systems – the DP Manager may know that if he does not provide facilities for 'end-user computing' on the company mainframe there will be an uncontrollable proliferation of microcomputers.

The option to choose application generators is itself one of the changes: their use is becoming much more widespread. Organisations that do not take advantage of the productivity gains that can be achieved in this way will carry a larger DP overhead than necessary, which could lead to their own demise. This book shows what organisations can realistically hope to achieve today and indicates the directions in which development is likely to go in the near future.

Another important area in which the current method of producing systems shows weaknesses is its lack of responsiveness to change. Even though it is possible to 'design for change' (Longworth, 1985), there are still unexpected changes which cause problems. Application generators offer a means of escape from the 'maintenance morass', because it can be simpler to make changes and then regenerate the system incorporating these changes.

It is sensible to consider the data processing scene in terms of the sorts of system which are likely to be encountered. These will vary from large systems involving high volumes of data which cover the day-to-day running of the company to what are in effect personal systems which affect the work of only a single person. In between, of course, there is a whole variety of systems which, though not vital to the company as a whole, are of the utmost importance to a group within it. These three types of system have been called *corporate, departmental* and *personal* and it may help to think of them in these terms. In the 'corporate' area there are most likely to be particular needs for processing efficiency to cope with the volumes of transactions that are involved. If anything goes wrong one needs to provide good levels of security to ensure recovery without the need to input a large amount of data again.

For an application generator to be of use in this area, it too must provide the same level of security. In fact there are application generators which provide this, though they will normally require DP experts to make the best use of their facilities. Where users are writing their own systems, it is more likely that they will be producing reports on data within the system than devising applications which update the company database. Some large-volume systems (particularly reporting systems) are low-risk because copies of their input files exist elsewhere, whereas personal files might hold details of company plans for the next five years and be of considerable value. The generators used for such systems must provide the requisite degree of security. Too much is better than too little but will inevitably be more expensive in resources.

As one moves down the scale of risk to 'departmental' systems, one discovers that the reduction in the critical nature of the work means that the systems are generally smaller and very much suited to current application generators. They may involve daily transactions but not in the volumes which require the level of integrity and efficiency described above. Tools suited to this type of system will also be usable by smaller companies for more of their work because they do not have the same volumes of data: the work is still critical to the running of the organisation but with fewer problems of recovery. The technical reasons for the suitability or otherwise of particular classes of application generator are explored below.

In addition there are many applications which can be treated as 'personal' systems. There is no danger to the organisation if the system goes down. The individual normally looks after security by taking copies of data from time to time, as would be done on a standalone microcomputer (there is conceptually very little difference between the mainframe-based personal system and a microcomputer system and cost may influence selection). Here there is usually no requirement by the user for any particular degree of computer efficiency providing the response time is not too degraded. Even so, the cumulative effect of a large number of such systems can impact on the overall load of the computer, especially on the central mainframe. This can be a complaint of those who have to take responsibility for capacity planning of computer networks where there is a significant load of 'personal' systems. The impact is seen both in terms of central processor usage and in the amount of disk storage required (it is a problem to make certain that personal users tidy up the files which they no longer need). Some organisations attempt to cater for this by setting up penalties within their charging algorithms. This can however penalise also those who need larger volumes of data.

WHY INTRODUCE APPLICATION GENERATORS?

There are many reasons why organisations should choose to use application generators. Even within the same organisation different people, with different needs, will give different reasons. However, many common themes have emerged and it is therefore worth trying to discover the patterns. (The reasons are explored in more detail in Chapter 3 when the experiences of user organisations are discussed.) The most common reasons are:

- to overcome shortcomings in existing systems – especially where difficulty is found in maintaining COBOL or assembler programs, because they are either particularly complicated or badly written;
- to avoid the difficulty of handling the intricacies of the teleprocessing monitor. It is said that some products are particularly useful for isolating the programmers from teleprocessing difficulties;
- to produce systems more quickly without sacrificing efficiency;
- to reduce labour costs by employing fewer programmers;
- to be able to react quickly to user demands;
- to allow users access to their own data;
- to write prototypes for reasons such as allowing the users to see, at the earliest possible stage in the design process, what the system may be like;
- to make the development process much more evolutionary. The application generator liberates the developers from the need to set up a monolithic system that it is impossible to change;
- to save on the chore of producing documentation and even systems specifications, by making the application generator output part of the system documentation;
- to reduce the amount of subsequent maintenance;
- to make it easier to modify systems as a response to changing business needs.

Organisations not intending to use fourth-generation languages declare that their present methods produce systems that are productive enough. Moreover, to introduce new methods would – certainly in the short term – dilute the effort available, because of the need for retraining. In addition it would make less efficient use of the computer and thus lead to greater costs. Also the increased use of application generators by users would lead to an uncontrollable explosion in the disk storage and processor capacity required. This important area is explored in more detail later with attention to the factors that need to be considered when deciding whether to make the change to application generators. Much depends on the organisation's needs as well as on its current use of hardware and software. Surveys have shown an increase in the number of those either using application generators now or contemplating their use. For example, the 1985 Urwick/*Computing* Survey showed that 45% of the respondents were already using fourth-generation languages to some extent and that another 32% were considering such a policy.

SOFTWARE ENGINEERING

Much stress is now rightly placed on the need for better engineering of software. Some believe that the use of application generators is not possible within an engineered environment, because the user of application generators is unwilling to tolerate engineering constraints. In fact there should be no conflict, so long as the life-cycle model is modified to take advantage of the productivity tool, as discussed in Chapter 6.

Engineering disciplines, based on proven theory, use well-established techniques and methods (both technical and managerial); and *tools* are extensively used both to gain accuracy and to assist in the performance of repetitive and mundane tasks. *Project control* is achieved by careful monitoring of the output of each phase of development – from initial requirement, sketches, blueprints, prototypes, etc, to production and testing. *Software engineering* is concerned with applying engineering techniques to software. The Open University MSc course defines software engineering as "the systematic application of an appropriate set of techniques to the whole process of software development".

One problem in integrating an application generator with software engineering is that to engineer software demands very highly structured methods, whereas the use of application generators is often less well structured (it is not known at the outset how many iterations of the prototype will be needed, so accurate estimates cannot be made). Another problem is that, with application generators, a number of the checks and balances likely to be used with larger teams are avoided: where one person can design and write a whole system and test it, there are possibilities of errors which might escape detection. (This is quite apart from the possibility of fraud, another consideration.)

Should such worries be allowed to discourage the use of application generators? In fact they can be used in a disciplined way within a structured framework, so long as precautions are taken. It is recommended that:

— application generators should be used within a structured framework such that it is possible to monitor the output of each phase of development;

— the life-cycle model will have to be modified to take account of the use of the new productivity tools. Thus parts of the normal design and implementation phases will appear to be bypassed;

— prototyping be used as an appropriate technique. (More is said later about the suitability of an application generator for prototyping.) This must be accomplished within an agreed framework so that the effect on the whole project can be properly controlled;

— the checks and balances must be put back in. The code written can be checked by another person and the whole test plan can be monitored by someone other than the original programmer. Reviews and inspections can be carried out with application generators, as with any other programming language.

More is said about control and standards in Chapter 6.

APPLICATION GENERATORS AND STRUCTURED METHODOLOGIES

Here there are two opposing problems. On the one hand the use of the structured methodology may be prescribed as a standard, needed to satisfy the demand for engineering principles to be used;

on the other, the organisation will not get the required productivity improvements if the structured methodology requires too much time to be spent on the design.

It is certainly recommended that a proper analysis of the data should be carried out. The structured methodology will help here. For example, SSADM (Structured Systems Analysis and Design Method) is being extended to include what is known as the 'fast-path' approach which bypasses some of the stages of the full version. CCTA (Central Computer and Telecommunications Agency) has produced some guidelines for the use of SSADM with application generators (CCTA, 1984). Here it is suggested that a formal structure will probably be required for large projects but less often for smaller ones. This is because:

— there is less need, with a small project, to develop and agree a firm user requirement at the earliest stage. It can follow a prototyping exercise using the application generator, if this aids understanding;

— there is more scope for iteration, backtracking and prototyping with an application generator;

— it is more difficult to separate the specification, design and development stages;

— the use of an application generator typically gives rise to less formal documentation – there may be no need for a program specification, if sufficient other information is embedded in the application code;

— the incremental development and delivery of functions introduces a non-sequential mode of staging the progress of the project. This should not imply that a lax approach is recommended: there is still need for project planning.

The recommended way of working with application generators for smaller projects, especially where one person is working individually on the job, is to carry out a data analysis exercise and then use the documentation facilities offered by the product. From then on, it is found that the generator documentation will automatically be kept up-to-date by subsequent amendments. It is very important that major changes should not be made to the system without making sure that they are also reflected in *all* the system documentation.

Few problems are anticipated with the smaller systems; more trouble may be found with larger systems because of the difficulty of control. It is felt however that this problem is not really to be laid at the door of the application generator. Perhaps, on occasion, too much stress has been put on the words 'self documenting' and this has led people to hope for too much.

APPLICATION GENERATORS AND TESTING

Is it any more difficult to test systems written with the aid of application generators? One large problem occurs where one has to treat the whole application as a 'black box' since one does not have access to any compiled code in a language that can be checked. This is not *that* different from the standard compilers and utilities which people have been using quite happily for many years. But of course there is a difference: a compiler must adhere to a published standard which can be monitored for conformance and certificated.

In the case of the fourth-generation languages of this type, one has to have faith in functional testing – one must test for all the things that the system is supposed to perform. It is more difficult to test for those things that the system ought *not* to do. With a 'coverage analyser' for a COBOL program one has some hope of finding those lines of code that have never been tested. Application generators do not have such facilities except where they produce COBOL code, though some do provide other debugging aids.

One advantage however is that fewer lines of code have been written (by a factor of up to ten, according to some people) and for this reason the testing is often found to be simpler. Since many functions that one might have to write using a third-generation language have been included in the generator, one knows that they will always operate in the same way. It is advisable to make sure that the supplier of the software has tested it properly since he does have the code. (There is a case here for independent tests of the quality of software.)

What one is able to do more easily – because there are fewer lines – is to study the code in the application generator to ensure that there are no hidden 'bombs' (which might be activated at some future date) or unexpected action codes (which might trigger unwanted effects). There is also a need for proper procedures to check on unauthorised access to the system. It may be that compiled code with proper control over the compilation process (ie version control and library procedures) is safer in this respect than interpreted code with no check on whether it has been altered since the previous time of running. One must control changes to the system, both to protect the users from unexpected results and also to protect the organisation from fraud – of course this will depend on the critical nature of the systems themselves.

Another approach is to see whether the application generator uses constructs within its language which can be directly related to the constructs of structured programming. James Martin, for example, follows this line of enquiry, translating the constructs into action diagrams (Martin, 1985).

3 User Needs and Experiences

USER NEEDS

Users of application generators may be divided into three classes:

Experts and regular developers – those using application generators as their main development language.

End-users writing their own systems – for the most part users making use of application generators to produce systems for their own use. This class can include also those using them to make enquiries on files and databases.

End-users of the system – those who employ the systems written by others with application generators. These people must not be forgotten so it is proper to consider the user-friendliness of the finished systems; users do not want to be forced to use systems that are not suitable any more than the developers wish to be forced to produce systems that are not easily usable.

There will always be overlaps between the first and second classes since there will be some 'users' who are more expert than some DP development staff. Naturally both classes should be considering the needs of the end-users of the systems which they produce, which means that the needs of the third class should always be looked after.

Experts and Regular Developers

Expert developers will very often be writing what one might call 'real' data processing systems, with large files of data and complicated processing to carry out. They therefore need powerful ways of handling data – which is why the use of application generators is seen as an answer to their requirements. And with reference to the man/machine interface, they may well find that the facility to write commands and command strings gives them more direct control over the development process than does the use of menus or prompted replies to questions posed by the application generator.

Since they are producing systems which interact with, and allow updating of, the organisation's main files, a number of features will be required to support this activity. In particular there will be a need (or at least a desire) for:

— means to carry out stringent validation of input data (against edit patterns, data types and tables);

— means of providing audit trails and other facilities acceptable to the internal and external auditors. This may include transaction logging;

— file handling features which ensure that the integrity of the database and all files is properly maintained at all times, such as checkpoints for restarting, record locking during updates, and logical transactions;

— the ability to design screen layouts to suit the application and its end-users rather than the generator. Against this it may be argued that on occasions programmers struggle to fit a preconceived screen design (or other design feature) into the application generator framework, whereas they should know how the generator wants them to carry out the processing. Care is required in deciding how much freedom is to be allowed. Many application generators do provide sufficient freedom for the programmer (see Chapter 4);

— means of carrying out logical processes, as with procedural logic in languages such as COBOL. A number of different ways of providing this are described in Chapter 4;

— the facility of going direct to particular screens without needing to go through the same sequence of other screens each time;

— means of file and database handling which deal with

complicated file structures and which allow selection and updating of matching records on other files;

— the ability to write 'programs', either by putting together files of commands or by using a special version of the language. One possible alternative is to embed the application generator commands within a language like COBOL, BASIC or FORTRAN, but this is not very attractive as it loses many of the benefits of using the application generator;

— documentation aids such as cross-reference lists;

— tuning features for file and database access.

It should also be noted that there will be many systems developed by data processing staff for which the languages described in the next sub-section will be quite adequate.

End-users Writing their own Systems

Where end-users produce their own systems, they are unlikely to be writing 'critical' systems, so the degree of security and control will not be so vital. Where users are in fact writing critical systems, some of the facilities listed above will be required, so the people concerned must be able to cope with them. (They should therefore refer to the section above.) For the most part, with this sort of user, one will require a much simpler interface with the computer. There are a number of ways in which this can be provided, such as:

— giving appropriate user-interface mechanisms such as menus and prompted responses. A more constrained approach allowing less freedom to the user may be appropriate. Assistance in the form of 'help' screens and messages is also useful;

— only permitting the simpler programming constructs. Either one should choose a language which does not contain the more complicated processing or one does not teach the extra commands to more naïve users;

— restricting the number of files which can be open at any one time; there will in any case be less need for the sort of system which requires complicated file structures;

— not expecting the users to worry about efficiency; they should concentrate on getting a working system. It will still be advantageous if the generator itself is reasonably efficient in its use of computer resources;

— providing the organisational back-up in advice, consultancy, data control, access to data from other systems and training. The information centre concept is important here, and is discussed below. As with all systems development, how it is organised is vital.

End-users of the System

The end-user requires mainly a man/machine interface suited to his needs. Other factors are considered below in looking at the needs of the organisation as a whole. (The reader is also referred to Damodaran et al, 1980; and Watts, 1984.) The most important consideration is to make sure that there is not a mismatch between the abilities of the end-users and the interface provided. If the interface is made too simple, regular users are less happy; conversely, any irregular users need to have their use of the system made as easy as possible.

ASSESSING REAL NEEDS

The introduction of application generators should aim to meet real needs rather than simply to follow fashion. Later it is seen how particular organisations have assessed their needs and made their choice in this area: they have normally had a problem to solve and have therefore looked for a product that provides a solution. First it is proposed to explore in more general terms where application generators are likely to prove useful to the organisation, and in particular how they may help the development process. Let us then start by thinking about the *information centre* and the *development centre.*

The Information Centre

An information centre comprises a small number of experts in software products available to users (as discussed in Chapter 2). The experts are there to support the users but not to develop their systems for them. The information centre can be seen as one attempt to put development power into end-user departments as a solution to the problem of data processing productivity. After all, users should know what they want: to avoid translating this into terms which the data processing department understands should lead to more accurate systems that do the job that is really required. This certainly works well with enquiries and simple programs: some organisations prefer to restrict this activity to what can be done on personal microcomputers, especially with spreadsheets such as LOTUS 1-2-3. The point of allowing this sort of access on the mainframe may be to allow access to data held in the company databases or to allow sharing of programs and data between colleagues.

However, it is more doubtful that complex and vital systems can be produced by user staff. How much does it really cost to turn the accountant or purchasing officer into a really competent analyst/programmer? In some organisations this has been successfully carried out. Elsewhere there may be only one person who understands the programs – which leaves the organisation in a vulnerable position. Another problem may be that of finding a replacement for the innovator who moves on.

The Development Centre

In contrast, the development centre is much more akin to the traditional data processing department. It develops systems on behalf of the users. There are differences: one will not often find the same large teams that may have been used with languages like COBOL or PL/1. The use of application generators allows the development centre to respond much more quickly to users' requests. Use of prototyping allows the users to become fully involved at an early stage: this leads to fewer changes later when it is much more inconvenient. Also, the same sort of systems and programs that can be provided through 'information centre' channels can be provided by development staff.

The first decision must be what the uses of the application generator are likely to be. Will it be wanted for the development of major systems or for user support, whether this means letting the users write their own systems or writing the programs in the DP department for use by user departments? The need may be for a product or a mix of products that supports both these activities. This may depend partly on local 'culture', on the availability of staff of the right calibre, or on many other factors. A number of such factors are highlighted in the following discussions of user experience.

There are various possible reasons why users may choose not to go along with the fourth-generation language revolution. There are a number of important considerations:

- the initial cost of the software may not be offset by the likely savings;
- the cost of training (retraining) may be too high;
- the effect on other development plans may be too disruptive;
- the ongoing costs of running fourth-generation language applications may be too high;
- there may not be enough terminals (and other hardware) for the users, so that the costs of introduction would be high.

Failure of an application generator may be due to some of the above economic factors, to the wrong choice of product, or to the wrong organisational structure.

OTHER NEEDS

Items such as the following will form prerequisites in the evaluation process (see also Chapter 5):

- matching existing hardware and operating system software;
- completing a particular project in a given time;
- saving a given percentage of development staff;
- not using more than x% extra hardware;
- fitting in with existing systems (this may involve consideration of file formats, languages, etc);
- having sufficient control over reporting and output screen formats to enable systems to be tailored to the requirements of the user, not the language;
- matching a particular design methodology (such as SSADM), and fitting into current development strategies;
- having portability, over a given range of hardware (to aim for portability as an *unspecific* ideal is not realistic).

It is also wise to assess whether these are firm, absolute requirements that are unalterable. It may be advisable to go against a seemingly firm requirement: for example, to choose the software first and then the hardware. This is not always possible. At a later stage in the process of choice and acquisition it is desirable to check how well these needs have been met, or how well they are likely to be met, by particular languages. This is discussed below.

USERS' ASSESSMENT OF NEEDS

It is instructive to look at some extracts from documents produced by organisations during their evaluation of application generators.

Case 1

One company, looking for a development tool which would also provide query facilities for non-DP staff, included the following list of features to be considered:

- directly executable tasks, in order to improve the productivity of programming staff;
- support for all of a given manufacturer's database products;
- possible links to other (specified) database products;
- availability of suitable back-up and security facilities for the files within the system;
- compatibility with a specific data dictionary;
- no prohibitive overheads on overall system throughput (no figures were specified at this stage, but all shortlisted products were to be put through the same test);
- control of access so that only specific individuals can get hold of authorised information, with special emphasis on updates.

Case 2

Another company was looking for a complete database system which would include a fourth-generation language. This meant that, in contrast to Case 1, they were much more interested in machine efficiency than in a particular level of staff productivity. Their own report stated that a fourth-generation language was an essential feature which must have screen formatting capabilities. Another consideration was that it was seen as preferable that the developed application should run as a free-standing application rather than under the continued control of the application generator. It was seen as useful rather than essential that it should be possible to access data on non-database files.

Case 3

Another organisation, a local authority, required a product that would address the problems of the development centre, but did not need a language able to provide a very high volume of transactions. This started to narrow the choice. Lists were also made of desirable features and technical considerations:

Desirable facilities:

- prototyping facilities;
- systems development without detailed program specifications;
- self documenting;
- on-line and batch;
- consistency between mainframe and micro-based systems;
- logical definition and redefinition of files;
- effective recovery and data security;
- testing and debugging aids;
- controlled amendments to be made easily and swiftly.

Technical requirements:

- to run on mainframe under particular operating system. Also micro version if possible;
- support of particular terminal types and file/database software;
- user exits to high-level language.

These requirements were used in the process of drawing up a short-list of thirteen products, which were swiftly reduced first to five and then to two products, which were subjected to a more stringent evaluation process.

Case 4

Another large organisation, aiming to provide a service which would connect a number of sites using different IBM operating systems, set the need to deal with specific operating systems and file access methods high on its list of priorities. The following features were also required:

— the ability to update more than one file from a single screen;
— business graphics;
— security and integrity;
— financial modelling and statistics;
— natural language interface for occasional users.

The company was looking for a product to provide *most* of these facilities, rather than expecting to find them all in the same application generator.

Case 5

Another organisation, a software house providing business solutions to clients' problems, needed a product that was portable over a wide range of hardware. This is quite different from the normal case where it is merely a *desirable* option (even though there is no intention to use the portability provided).

Case 6

One organisation evaluated a fourth-generation language but then decided against purchase – because they could not estimate the likely cost savings. They were unable to put a financial value on the information that would be provided and were not immediately envisaging any savings in development staff (though they hoped that they would be able to provide interrogation facilities on relational files). The whole decision process rested ultimately on this one important point.

It is clear that organisations are trying to match the product with the type of user and the intended use. In the large mainframe environment, people are looking for products which are suitable in either the information centre, where users are writing their own systems with back-up from advisors and technical experts, or the development centre, comprising DP staff engaged in developing systems on behalf of their users. One also has to look to the differences in the type of systems which will be produced, particularly to ensure that transaction processing systems with high volumes of data are produced in a language which runs efficiently enough and has the necessary features to provide security against disaster (such as logging, recovery, checkpoint restart and record locking to prevent concurrent access).

On minicomputers too there are differences between the available fourth-generation languages, which may make one language more suitable for a given application or use than another. For example, the user interface and the permitted file structures together may make a product suitable only for straightforward systems. One product has an excellent keypad-driven interface which is very powerful for looking at and updating single records (in particular, with facilities for browsing backward and forward, and various selection modes). It is however much less flexible where more than one file needs to be handled. A decision may have to be made as to whether one is going to need to access files from more than one application or will find self-contained systems satisfactory.

EXPERIENCES OF USER ORGANISATIONS

General

Hard work is involved in making a success of the introduction of application generators. User experience indicates gains that can be made in addition to the productivity advantages that stem from the use of these tools.

In the evaluation stage one needs some knowledge of the application generator market. Even when using consultants or other advisors, there is still the need for enough knowledge to understand the consultants' report; to ensure, for example, that they do not suggest a product to satisfy a non-existent need.

When an organisation has decided to purchase an application generator, skills are needed to use the product to the full:

organisational, training and planning skills are necessary for the product to be effectively introduced to the department.

There is the need to learn how to tune the application generator in order to make it as efficient as possible: this may involve systems programmers who might otherwise not be involved. There are likely to be areas where knowledge and skills can be developed to make the best use of the product, such as the design of systems and data to suit the particular idiosyncracies of the software. It is to be assumed also that the organisation will wish to keep up-to-date with developments, both in the language in use and in the area generally. It should also be remembered that the estimating of new systems should be based on new figures. These statistics must therefore be built up from the first applications with the new language and incorporated in a formula which every developer can use. It may therefore be found useful to build into such a formula a comparison with COBOL or whatever language was previously in use.

Experiences Reported by Organisations

The experiences described should indicate the sort of changes that installing an application generator can make, though not all these changes can be expected at every site. If beneficial, the can be planned for; if unwelcome, they can be guarded against. The effects are often independent of the product in use. In any event, the particular effects must be set against the reasons for the choice of product.

Productivity/Economics

There are organisations where it is now general policy to use the application generator for all new development. Indeed one local authority has stated that not only new systems but also enhancements to existing systems (wherever possible) must be developed using a fourth-generation language. Their pilot schemes having produced savings of about a half in development costs and timescales, they are expecting to balance any extra costs due to the new software's known inefficiency by (a) producing it more effectively, (b) reducing processing costs with a new mainframe at a proportionately lower rental, and (c) phasing out a number of products currently in use. This is only possible because their only high-volume financial systems had been developed using packaged software (and are exempt from the policy above). Thus most other systems are of a small or medium size and therefore suitable for development in the particular application generator chosen.

Where an application generator is introduced into a large organisation which has a considerable quantity of data processing systems already, it may take some time before the percentage of slightly more inefficient systems becomes sufficient to become really noticeable. This gives sufficient time to adjust to the new regime.

Efficiency/Use of Machine Resources

Any organisation with an already critical loading on its computers should consider carefully the effect of introducing a fourth-generation language. Some companies have favoured minicomputers here, because each major application is expected to justify the cost of both hardware and software in the same proposal. The additional cost of hardware to carry the application generator might be cancelled out by the savings in development time and there can be no disadvantageous effect on other systems, as might have been the case if all had been running on the same mainframe.

One software house found it economic to write bespoke software in a fourth-generation language because the overall cost of the hardware/software package was less. They were also able to justify any additional running costs.

The efficiency of a fourth-generation language might sometimes depend on the mix of applications. Different sources state that the same product (a) costs twice as much to run and is notoriously greedy in its use of disk storage, and (b) is only about 14% less efficient than the previous COBOL programs, using the same database as before. Efficiency also depends on the nature of the application: application generators are often poor on heavy calculations and good on input/output to screens, whereas the efficiency of input/output to files depends on the indexing mechanism in use and the length of the database access paths.

Failures

Few failures are reported, perhaps because of the natural reticence of the people involved. One organisation, enthusiastic at the evaluation stage, discovered during pilot projects that there were problems in using the application generator with a particular operating system. Clearly the evaluation was inadequate. In another situation the 'front runner' after the first stage of the evaluation did very well until subjected to a test involving realistic files with an operational volume of data to process, at which point the response time went down to an unacceptable level: the vendor was given every opportunity to improve this but in the end the generator had to be rejected, despite its superiority in other spheres.

Specific Experiences

Experiences can usefully be subdivided into those of DP practitioners and those of end-users. It is perhaps inevitable that most of the views published are those of the data processing community: even where one does talk to users, the meeting has very often been arranged by the DP side. It is still helpful to find that all the users interviewed were pleased with what they had seen of fourth-generation languages.

The Experiences of Data Processing Personnel

The people whose experiences are described here ranged from data processing managers to programmers with only a very few years' experience. It was found that they had a clearer idea (than the end-users) of what to expect, and that these expectations were often met by the products chosen. In general they were favourably disposed to the products, having some minor criticisms of the technical working of the languages, but mostly coping with the limitations.

Relations with End-users

Some of the most favourable reactions came in relation to the improved contact with the end-users. A number of reasons were given for this, ranging from the dialogue facilitated by the prototyping process to the fact that systems were now completed faster (it was not necessary to refuse the user so often, when he requested an extra report, a system modification, etc).

Development Productivity

At some sites the DP staff could be sure that they had achieved their objectives. Here they had taken steps to measure what they were achieving before and after the introduction of the application generator. It is true that they were only able to compare accurately figures for very small pilot systems, since they had not made a practice of programming a system of any size in both the application generator and COBOL or PL/1 or whatever other language had previously been in use. Some figures are included in Figure 3.1. It will be seen that some of the comparisons are between actual figures (for the application generator) and estimates (for the COBOL): it is not felt that this invalidates the comparisons. Since the estimates are known to be correct within a reasonable degree of accuracy, the use of such estimates does not alter the relative values of the ratios produced.

Lines produced	PRODUCT A	COBOL	
Example 1	14650	58000 (e)	
Example 2	3550	12000 (e)	
Man hours (including some prototyping): the following figures include the analysis, design, coding and testing phases			
Example 3	2073	4923	1:2.4
Example 4	3058	10900 (e)	1:3.6
Benchmark (without prototyping), ie coding and testing only			
Example 5	65	463	1:7

Note: (e) indicates an estimated figure

Figure 3.1
Productivity Gains from Use of an Application Generator

Application generator comparison experiments have been carried out by the Central Computer and Telecommunications Agency for the government. They have written the same system using a number of application generators to enable detailed comparisons to be made. The results (published as an internal report – CCTA, 1984; and summarised in Appendix 3 of the present book) are instructive, but suffer from one drawback: the generators would not be chosen in a real evaluation because they could perform the particular task chosen as the benchmark. These results should be studied with care. It must also be remembered that these experiments were not carried out by programmers already expert in the languages in question but by people specially trained for the purpose.

Staff Attitudes

One possibility, only encountered on one occasion, is that programming staff who felt that their skills were being downgraded might resort to overt or covert obstruction. It has been said, for example, that it is easier to train new graduates than to retrain programmers. Some organisations are however worried that their programmers may decide to change jobs if they find the new products less of a challenge (see also Chapter 6).

Experiences of End-users and Managers

The following statements were made by end-users with regard to the use of application generators. No exhaustive study has been performed, so these statements are indicative rather than definitive.

A company director.

> "I run my business with the help of the computer systems which are in use. A 4GL helped me to put in completely new systems in 9 months and therefore this development contributed to profits 15 months earlier than would have been the case with previous development strategies."

A departmental manager.

> "Putting in minor changes, even at late stages of the development, has not been a problem like it used to be when specifications were frozen before the design was coded." This statement was followed by an interjection from the accompanying O & M Officer (who was a member of the Management Services Department). "The users still have to be controlled to prevent them from making too many late changes. But we both remember when we used to introduce manual override procedures because we could not change the computer systems."

A chief executive.

> "We have been very keen to embrace the new ideas. When we introduced this package, we were hoping to attack the considerable backlog which we knew to exist. We have not succeeded in

doing this and are glad, because what we have done is to find what people's real problems were and have written smallish systems to deal with them."

A clerical officer.

"The main gains have been that we have been able to learn how to access the data and write our own reports, and secondly that we have had very good co-operation from the development function in getting things to look how we really want them."

In general the comments of most users of systems have been favourable. It is quite apparent that they find the timely production of systems, and the chance to become more closely involved, to be major gains.

4 Features

INTRODUCTION

A comprehensive list of features (as in Appendix 2) can be used selectively as a reference checklist but is less practical for someone currently evaluating application generators with a view to purchase or use. This is because it is often a combination of features that a particular user needs, and in any case there are other attributes which must be examined first (see Chapter 5). In such a mammoth compendium of features one could only begin to indicate which were really needed and which were merely nice to have.

It is therefore certain that a more selective examination will be useful to more people. This chapter looks at the most typical features as well as some noteworthy variations. As a result, the prospective purchaser should be helped to ask the right sort of questions, to look at demonstrations critically, and to understand brochures and manuals.

FEATURES

The following topics are discussed:

- architecture: classifying application generators;
- compilation or interpretation;
- data dictionaries;
- input features:
  - the man/machine interface;
  - the development process;
  - getting data into the system;

- processing and logic;
- files and databases:
  - existing applications;
  - efficiency;
  - access control and security;
  - flexibility;
- output features.

Architecture: Classifying Application Generators

There are four overlapping classes of application generators which one can classify partly in terms of the functions they possess but also in terms of the uses for which they are suitable:

1 General-purpose application generators.
With these one would expect to be able to design and program a very large proportion of any application which could have been produced using a third-generation language such as COBOL.

2 Relational models.
There are a number of products which are based more or less closely on relational architecture; the system is defined in terms of its entities and the relationships between them. Such a product will be particularly useful where the system requirements and design have been defined in these terms. It will be found that more products are becoming available to provide direct links between structured design methods and application generators.

3 Languages for 'transaction-based' systems.
Some application generators are particularly suited to the production of transaction-based data processing systems; their internal framework treats the processing as a sequence of message exchanges which is particularly suitable for such systems. They also produce systems which are more efficient in their use of the computer than those produced with general-purpose application generators. The other advantage of using such software is that it does not normally require the same level of technical knowledge as the manufacturer's own teleprocessing software. This means that systems can be built by programmers with less experience.

4 Generators suitable for end-user systems.
Either the whole application generator, or more often a subset of it, can be made available for end-users to write their own systems. Such software must provide an interface which is very easy to use without extensive knowledge or training. This is accomplished in one of the following ways:

— by providing a series of menus which give clear indications of what can be done;

— by leading the programmer more directly through the series of operations that have to take place in order to produce the system;

— by providing a natural language for queries;

— by providing access to a display of the fields on a file and letting the users select in turn those that they wish to see displayed; they can also indicate which fields will be used to sort the file and where control breaks and sub-totals will occur;

— by having standard update and enquiry utilities for use on single files.

Compilation or Interpretation

Application generators generate their systems in different ways. In all cases there must be a translation process between the language which the programmer uses and the machine code on which the computer operates. There are two main options, compilation or interpretation, with a number of intermediate positions. Precisely the same is seen with third-generation languages; for example, COBOL code must be put through a compiler to produce the object code which forms the run-time system. With BASIC or APL a different process is often employed whereby each line of code is converted to the machine code as it is interpreted at run time.

Thus in the 'compiled' mode, the whole program is converted as a block into the set of machine code instructions. If a change has to be made, it must be made to the COBOL statements and the whole program must be recompiled. In the 'interpreted' mode however, there is also the option, during the development process, of adding lines or changing their contents and then rerunning. The critical difference is that one may rerun the set of instructions, changed slightly, with only the minimum of delay.

The alternative modes offered with application generators are:

— full compilation
In this case the whole application has to be compiled as a single entity. This may be done by having the application generator itself produce COBOL code to be read through a standard compiler, or there may be a specific compiler for the application generator's own language. There will be advantages in run-time efficiency, at the cost of slowing the development process. Another possible advantage is that the code produced may be portable onto a different target machine, ie any machine with a suitable compiler.

— part compilation
Many components of the language are precoded and can thus be called up as required. The whole system is in fact built up as a series of small programs, each consisting of no more than about fifty lines of code. Some of these programs will need no compilation because they are full of standard components, others will need compiling after changes because of the effect on data addressing in particular. This will however only affect the immediate program which can thus be compiled in a matter of seconds, which gives this mode some of the advantages of both the 'compiled' and 'interpreted' modes. This is very similar to the case where all functions are precoded and chosen by means of table entries built up during the system construction phase. This may be more efficient because no compilation needs to take place, but some changes will still affect data addresses.

— interpretation
In this mode each line of code has to be read and translated in turn, whether the input is an existing file written previously or is being typed at a terminal for immediate execution. This is very flexible during the development process as additional facilities can very easily be added, but at a cost of the overhead of interpretation whenever the system is used.

— hybrid
Some application generators overcome this last problem by

having both modes available, the 'interpreted' mode for development and a compiler to produce a more efficient run-time system.

Data Dictionaries

All application generators rely on a data dictionary or directory. This stores details of what data fields are available to the system and provides a measure of data independence as the dictionary entry can be changed without seriously affecting the programs, so long as the field still exists. Such changes may involve recompilation.

The simpler products use the data dictionary in a passive way, as a repository of information only. It holds details of what is available which such information as field size and type and also column headings to be used on reports.

Further facilities available on more sophisticated products include validation rules such as range checks or table-look-up checks. Sometimes additional data types can be specified to cater for the requirements of the application, for example to handle a code which contains a mixture of alphabetical and numeric characters.

More dynamic use of a data dictionary is seen where the control over the data is such that the user cannot attempt to use a field not present on the data dictionary and the deletion of a dictionary entry is not possible where there are existing usages of the field in question. There are also data dictionaries which hold details of 'views'; that is, where a set of related fields is designated as available to a certain class of user. It is a very good security feature to ensure that sensitive data is not available to unauthorised persons.

Although most application generator products contain their own data dictionaries, it can also be beneficial to have access to proprietary data dictionary products which are already in use within the organisation. Some products contain the requisite links.

Input features

The Man/Machine Interface

The man/machine interface can affect the use of application generators in two ways. Firstly it affects the development process in the form of the dialogue employed by the designer or programmer in making the product provide the system that is required. Secondly, it also clearly affects the completed system and the way it is used.

Here it is the developers who are to be considered and it will be their responsibility to provide systems which are suitable for their eventual users. It has already been seen in studying the 'architecture' how some products are designed to produce efficient transaction-based systems, in that they provide a dialogue consisting of 'message pairs' which is particularly suitable for this type of on-line system. Other application generators provide facilities which make it easy to set up control structures based largely on menus, which will be good for many applications whose users are not using them all the time with large volumes of data where the menus might become an impediment to efficiency. All these topics will have to be considered when choosing an application generator.

The Development Process

Different styles of input are used by different application generators. It is clearly worthwhile looking for the style which suits the development staff and environment. In addition, it is necessary to consider other factors which make one product easier to learn and use than another, such as:

— the quality of the documentation provided with the product, such as the user manuals and training material;

— the ease of access to and understanding of 'help' facilities and error messages;

— any use of control characters or control keys, which may conflict with existing practice and therefore be potentially confusing;

— the quality of the 'editor' provided with the software.

The following are the most common of the styles which are found:

— command-based
Many languages are controlled using a command-based syntax. The commands may include both procedural and non-procedural elements according to the processing required. There will be differences in the number and power of the commands. The commands themselves are not always

rigid; for example, abbreviation of commands and keywords may be permitted and there may be optional words in the syntax. In general this style suits those with some programming background.

— menu-controlled
The options are here displayed in the form of a series of menus. This reduces the number of items that need to be memorised, which aids developers who have less experience or use the application generator less frequently. It can however become irksome to those carrying out large developments. For this reason this style is sometimes offered as an alternative input style which can be used as appropriate.

— parameter-driven
Here structured input screens are provided for the developer to make the selections which control the final system. After providing answers and filling in boxes on these screens the system is generated. Sometimes, in order to make the development process less prone to error, the sequence of screens must follow the set pattern. If this means that the full sequence must be followed whenever changes, even minor ones, have to be made, this can lead to frustration.

— positional
Some generators rely on the positional placing of items on the screen, such as commands, logical selection or field selection. This works very well in direct on-line mode and has been used in a number of very large on-line systems. If this requires a separate control language to convert the screens into command files to be saved and reused, this control language must also have a good user interface.

Getting Data into the System

There may be a standard utility to make it easy to put data into a single file or to update it. Such utilities often list the fields down the screen in the order specified to the data dictionary, making very few concessions to either elegance or the convenience of the user. It is therefore more likely to be useful for the input of data to test the system than in the final system, where considerations of data security or access control may well rule out the utility. It is also likely that the validation which can be carried out by the utility is limited, unless there is a very good linkage with a powerful data dictionary.

For this reason, on most systems it is necessary for people to develop their own input programs, using input mechanisms such as screen painting or specifying screen co-ordinates, as discussed above. This will also make possible the use of more complicated validation, the use of multiple files within the update process and the acquisition of some data from other files and systems.

Processing and Logic

One of the benefits of application generators is that they can release the programmer from the need to write procedural logic in COBOL or PL/1. There are many different ways to accomplish this aim. They normally result from the fact that the application generator contains a built-in processing structure and this may in itself give rise to certain restrictions, such as where only a single file can be updated in a given transaction.

The following are some of the ways in which different application generators handle the problem of processing logic:

a) there may be a built-in processing structure, which ensures that the files are handled in a proper manner, ie controls the updating process according to its standard logic.

b) simple procedural code, eg constructs such as "IF...THEN... ELSE". In this case, the application generator may be providing its benefits in some other area rather than in the saving of procedural code.

c) by allowing 'logic' to be inserted at fixed points in the processing cycle, such as before and after each screen is displayed.

d) by allowing the user or developer to select records according to various criteria before the processing, whether updating or reporting, is carried out.

e) by means of decision tables inserted into the command or code structure.

f) by calling lower-level languages such as COBOL or BASIC from within the application generator. This is a very useful feature where it is included to allow routines for which the lower-level language is more suitable (eg complicated manipulation of statistics perhaps), but may be found restrictive if required for more basic logical selection.

g) writing programs in the lower-level language, but calling file handling from the application generator.

h) using built-in comparison functions already contained in the application generator.

Files and Databases

Although the choice of database software falls outside the scope of the current work, it is nevertheless important to discuss some of the links between application generators and databases. This helps to put into perspective the choices that have to be made.

Firstly it must be realised that some application generators are completely self-contained, with their own database structure, or are very closely linked to a particular database manager. Others use the computer manufacturer's standard file handling or database software.

Existing Applications

Wherever there is a large investment in existing programs and files, it is clearly important that the application generator should be able to link with the systems using these. This may dictate the database software that must be used (which will limit the choice of products considerably) or it may be found sufficient to ensure that the files written by existing systems can be read by the application generator and vice versa.

If the application generator uses the standard file handling software, it may be thought that this will mean that all files written by it will invariably be available to other systems. This is not however the case if, for example, the application generator uses its own algorithms for packing variable-length data records before writing them onto a file.

Efficiency

Files with large numbers of records or a high transaction rate will be best handled by an efficient database management system, particularly one in which there are facilities for tuning. Such tuning implies more than a casual knowledge of the database and may therefore require the specialist knowledge of a database administrator or systems programmer. Efficiency depends partly on the initial design of the database structures and access paths and partly on the tuning features – such as changing block sizes, adding more pointers (to make enquiries more efficient) or taking them out (to speed up the updates). Sometimes duplication of data, against the strict tenets of normalisation, is useful.

On occasions where an enquiry process is found to be particularly inefficient, it proves to be the initial selection of data (ie the access path chosen) which is at fault. An expert in the use of the application generator will be able to sort out such problems and for this reason the software support offered by the vendors is undoubtedly vital.

Access Control and Security

Control of access to data may be vital. For applications which are only used by one person, it may be sufficient to control access to the system itself, normally by password or straightforward administrative procedures. For multi-user systems, much more sophisticated controls are possible. For the integrity of the database, any record which is to be updated must be locked to prevent corruption by another person trying to update it at the same time. With more sensitive applications, data can be protected from unauthorised access at either file or field level. Some products permit users to look only at fields in 'views' of the data which they are authorised to see (a 'view' can include fields from a number of different files on a relational or other database).

Other features which protect the integrity of the database are the logging of transactions and possibly before- and after-images of the master record as well as audit files. These will be used for applications where the data cannot be recreated without inputting the transactions since the last security copy of the database for a second time. The frequency of taking such copies will depend on the activity on the file and how long one can afford to wait for the recovery process to take place.

Flexibility

One of the major advantages of application generators should be the ease of making changes to cater for alterations in business requirements. To cope with this it may be necessary to make changes to the database structure.

There are two effects to be considered:

— the effect on program logic
If fields are added it may make no difference to program logic or it may be necessary to recompile either part or all of the system. If fields have to be deleted, then all references to them have to be deleted too.

— the effect on data
Some products allow the addition of data fields and control references within the software. In other cases it will be necessary to carry out a reorganisation, perhaps by dumping the existing data and restoring it to take care of the changes. A good product will provide utilities to cater for the process of reorganisation. To make it easier to add fields during the cycle of prototyping or the earlier stages of design, some experienced designers allow for an expansion of 10% which can be deleted later if not required. This practice is most valuable with products which do not allow for the dynamic addition of fields.

Output Features

Most application generators include the basic features of both a query language and a report writer. In other words they allow the user both to make on-line enquiries and to produce printed reports, both on individual records and wider selections of data.

The reporting features of the application generator must allow it to produce various forms of output, including tabular reports with totals and multiple levels of subtotalling and averages, percentage calculations and counts of the number of occurrences of records; graphical representations of data may be of interest to some organisations. It is certainly desirable that one should be able to store report specifications for execution later.

For developers of systems the style of input must be compatible with that used for the input and processing parts of the language, in order to avoid confusion – not a problem for most application generators except where their various constituent parts have been derived from different sources. Writing commands which control the report is the most flexible mode for people with a programming background. A factor which should be considered is whether abbreviations can be used and whether the sequence of parameters is important.

Where users are likely to make ad-hoc queries or to write their own reports, they will need a style of input which suits them. A number of ways have been devised to avoid the need to learn the syntax of the report-writer. For example, one product has a front-end which displays the options which can be chosen as a series of menus from which the relevant parameters can be chosen and builds up from this the commands which the parent product needs. Another powerful way of avoiding the need to learn the commands required is to have an 'intelligent' program to interpret the input from the user and convert the less formal words which he might use – almost, but not quite, natural language – into the form which the generator can understand. There is of course a penalty to pay in terms of the efficiency of the system, and these front-end translators are most recommended where the investment can be justified in terms of time saved or information provided. The potential user needs to be warned about the dangers of misinterpreting data extracted in this way.

One difficulty that may well be encountered during the evaluation process is that it is easy to see that the basic reporting is carried out satisfactorily but one does not in fact know which options will be required in real life – the best advice here is to look at some typical reports from existing systems and to ask the supplier how his product would have coped, or to draw up a specification for the most important and most complicated reports that can be foreseen and to try this out during the evaluation period.

5 Choosing an Application Generator

THE EVALUATION PROCESS

In order to carry out a thorough evaluation of both the need for an application generator and the products to satisfy that need is not an easy task. Sometimes it is not carried out properly because the organisation has not been able to justify the expense, or because the first product seen satisfies some of the known needs. This can be a dangerous situation when some benefit is gained in the early stages (perhaps when simple systems are being designed) but when the product cannot provide the same pay-back on more critical systems. A better choice could often have been made with a proper approach to system selection.

This chapter aims to offer data processing organisations of all sizes a framework to help them make the right decisions. It will also enable them to face salesmen in a more positive manner, because it will help them to ask the right questions.

A MULTI-STAGE APPROACH

The recommended approach is to use a sequence of different tests or levels of test. On the first pass, after the needs have been defined, one identifies relevant products. The second pass looks more closely at those shortlisted to discover those which most closely match the requirements of the organisation. If necessary, an even more detailed examination is performed to make the final selection.

The four stages that are recommended are:

1 Discovery of the needs of the organisation to make sure that

only truly relevant products are evaluated. At the same time, a parallel activity might be undertaken, to carry out a survey of the application generator market.

2 The checking of all relevant products against the essential needs of the organisation, as discovered in Stage 1, in order to draw up a shortlist.

3 A paper evaluation of the products shortlisted, in order to find those which most closely match the predetermined needs of the organisation. This often depends on somewhat subjective comparisons. Nonetheless the evaluation approach recommended here helps the user guard against disastrous mistakes.

4 Practical testing of the software, whether to make the final selection or merely to check out the single surviving product. This might involve demonstrations by suppliers, prototype systems, programs with a real purpose. These may be undertaken either by the vendor or the purchaser of the software according to the resources and experience available.

NEEDS OF THE ORGANISATION

Here one is interested in relevant needs. What is sought is a statement of the immediate problems which have given rise to the need for an application generator, with as much analysis as necessary at this point in the cycle. This will become clearer as examples are discussed. At the same time the potential purchaser should begin to look at what application generators are currently able to offer.

The reason for this second part of the operation is that otherwise one could define the need for a type of product that could not possibly be produced or ignore certain functions that could in fact be available. For example, it would be quite senseless to specify a product that would increase programmer productivity by a factor of at least 200, if such a figure is in fact unattainable; it would however be eminently sensible to ask for a product which would offer the maximum possible increase in productivity, because this requirement would provide one good pointer to the type of product which was required.

Other possible reasons, which have already been discussed in Chapter 3, include:

— a desire for end-users to write systems of their own or to be given 'query language' facilities;

— the need to increase the speed of production of systems;

— saving the need to learn the manufacturer's teleprocessing monitor in detail – the application generator may provide its own environment;

— involvement of users in an evolutionary design process, with a product which both produces prototype systems quickly and also generates systems which are easy to change throughout their life;

— the desire to control documentation and simplify maintenance.

An informed knowledge of what is available in the marketplace is plainly an asset in this evaluation. A biased view based on knowledge of only a single product will hinder the correct choice. Nevertheless, where interest has been aroused by a particular product, this should be put through the same screening process as any other application generators discovered in the second stage of the evaluation process. In one case, the person who had started an investigation of fourth-generation tools was surprised that the product seen first (and 'sold' to him by an enthusiastic user) was not selected: it failed a number of his organisation's selection criteria.

The recommended approach can of course be used as a sort of defence mechanism during the purchasing process. With a complete list of requirements it is easier to argue constructively point by point.

The results of these deliberations should be written down in terms such as:

— this organisation needs a product that can produce efficient programs (no more than 20% less efficient than a COBOL program performing the same function) and it must be able to handle the throughput of transactions specified (in terms of the number per hour or whatever);

— the product must be usable by the clerks in the accounts department to carry out simple enquiries and to produce reports. It is more useful to be specific rather than to say 'end-users';

— it is essential that sensitive portions of personal data (eg salary or grade information) should be protected, ie only available to those authorised to see it. How this should be carried out is considered in detail later in this chapter.

This forms the first part of the list of requirements.

THE OPERATIONAL ENVIRONMENT

A second part of the list of requirements also needs to be determined before products can be shortlisted – this concerns the operational environment. The software selected may have to mesh with the operating system already in use, as well as with both existing and proposed databases, data dictionaries, file structures and other software systems. It must clearly be decided how far new systems must interact with the old.

This is an area in which the organisation can be constrained by its environment, but there are still choices or trade-offs to be made.

The following list of operational and other requirements was used by one organisation in their own evaluation of application generators.

— support for the manufacturer's strategic database and file handling products;

— compatible with suitable back-up and security facilities;

— compatible with specified data dictionary;

— simple and efficient screen and forms generation;

— has own query language or the ability to link with other enquiry languages;

— does not require a specific database product to function;

— can be used by end-users for development, or at least screen design;

— does not cause a prohibitive overhead on overall system throughput;

— can be integrated easily within the normal systems development life-cycles;

— is still being enhanced and guaranteed to have interfaces to future database products provided by the specified manufacturer.

In looking for a tool which was described as a 'fourth-generation application generator', it is perhaps obvious that reporting facilities were required. Nevertheless the complete list provided a framework for discussion at the outset and thus prevented the investigation from going down blind alleys. These discussions might for example have shown that the updating was much more critical than the enquiries or reports or, vice versa, that the updating could be carried out in batch mode overnight whereas the on-line enquiries would be vital to the users.

Other organisations, with different needs, have used different lists of requirements.

SHORTLISTING RELEVANT PRODUCTS

The most up-to-date sources should be used to discover candidate application generators to appear on a shortlist. The reader may find information about the products that are available from the following sources:

— 1985 Inbucon Survey (INBUCON 1985);

— IDPM Survey of Available Products (IDPM 1986B);

— other books (see bibliography);

— exhibitions; eg most of the available 4GLs for the DEC VAX are to be seen at the annual DEC User Show;

— software directories;

— the computer press, both news and advertisements;

— the computer manufacturers, who may offer either their own software or independent products on licence according to their policy on such matters;

— advice from consultants or software houses.

This section will give some assistance in reducing the list to a manageable number of real possibilities.

In this book it is assumed that it is already known on what hardware the software is required to run. Where this is not the case there is an even more complicated task in choosing the total hardware/software package. Where there are both hardware and software requirements to be considered, it will be necessary to include the parameters for the acquisition of the application generator in the total list of requirements to be met by the combined package. It is then assumed that the comparative evaluation of any application generators can be carried out in the way described in this chapter.

Even in the 'normal case', where the hardware is already decided, there are other considerations to be sorted out. It may be possible to do this in advance by putting down a suitable list of requirements, but it may need further discussions with particular vendors and perhaps the computer manufacturer to decide what are the advantages and disadvantages (in this particular case) of particular features of the product under review.

For example, when looking at the choice of database and file handling to be used alongside the application generator, there may be a number of routes that can be followed, each of which will have their individual advantages and disadvantages:

— the use of the manufacturer's own file handling software has been chosen by some software writers for the sake of standardisation and to make applications generated by the fourth-generation language easy to integrate with other systems. This is particularly advantageous where there already exists a good understanding of these file structures. Some organisations also like the fact that there are fewer overheads than with the use of database management software.

  When choosing this route, it is necessary to make sure that the product includes any features that have been stated as requirements, such as relational (or 'pseudo-relational' file handling, automatic logging and security of transaction data. One may indeed be causing more work if it means that such features are not automatic but require extra effort at the coding stage. If this is the case it will be necessary to ascertain how much work this involves and how secure the result will be. It may also be necessary to carry out trials to find this out;

— where the software includes its own database the questions are: what effect will this have on the import and export of data, and what implications are there for systems which wish to gain access to this data without recourse to the application generator? As with all such choices there will be gains and losses to be considered. Only the particular organisation making the choice can state what its needs are;

— the same considerations apply when there is a possibility of using a well-known proprietary database. Where a hierarchical database suits the structure of the data and the demands that will be made of it, this may be a good choice. It will be necessary to balance the overheads of using a database against its undoubted benefits in certain circumstances. It is likely that there will be many considerations well outside the scope of this book – what must be done is to learn what effect this choice will have on the application generator in particular. One question is whether there is true integration, such that both read and write functions can be carried out directly onto the database or whether there is merely an interface subroutine which can be used to gain communication between the two;

— one has to make the same decisions in relation to the choice of relational database products. Relational architecture is very suitable as a vehicle for the data to be processed by application generators; the simplicity of the tabular structure makes it easy to produce the reports and enquiries that are required. There are currently many reservations about the efficiency of relational databases, but it is likely that their efficiency will continue to improve. Not all of those products that claim to be relational are truly so, so it is essential to check what relational capabilities are in fact present and whether the full set of features is required.

For the purposes of the example used later in this chapter, the first of these options has been chosen.

At this stage in the selection procedure information can be obtained from sales literature (or other documentary sources), consultants, salesmen, exhibitions and demonstrations. A Software Tools Demonstration Centre has been set up, under the auspices of the Department of Trade and Industry, by the National Computing Centre. This offers unbiased advice.

In many cases it will be sufficient to consider in the first screening process only the essential features listed. Where this does not bring the number down to a manageable size, some consideration of the other features is needed. This might involve a first look at key features (which might include security, the reputation of the firm selling the product, price or support potential). Products can be eliminated if they do not appear likely to score highly on the desirable criteria.

The next (third) stage of evaluation is more labour-intensive and could take several days per product, even for someone who knows the area. Therefore there is a clear advantage in reducing the number of products to be dealt with. It should not be reduced too far in case something of importance is missed. A figure of between three and six would not be unreasonable. Where a 'front-runner' is available from more than one source, both suppliers may have to be considered. There are also cases where one vendor is in a position to supply two or more products; it should not automatically be assumed that he will be able to provide the same level of training and support with each.

Third Stage of Evaluation Process

Having sifted out products which do not meet essential criteria and then drawn up a shortlist, the more detailed evaluation can be conducted.

This detailed evaluation is itself a double operation. The first task is both to decide the questions that need to be asked and to assign to these the appropriate weighting values. Only then can the products be evaluated in detail and scores allocated.

In the following schema the questions to be asked of each product are allocated to categories, each of which makes its own individual contribution to the total. It is decided what value is to be given to, for example, 'security'. If this is going to be worth 20% to the organisation, the individual scores (marked out of 10) given to each answer are scaled to give this effect. The values should be considered afresh for each different organisation, according to its needs. In the current example the following contribution factors and values are used (they would be applicable to many organisations needing a general purpose application generator, which is why this has been chosen as an appropriate model):

1.	functionality	30%
2.	files	20%
3.	security	20%
4.	efficiency	10%
5.	support	5%
6.	reputation	5%
7.	portability	5%
8.	price	5%

Other organisations might perhaps rate efficiency more highly and might not find portability of any interest. Not everyone will agree that price should be included in the evaluation at this stage, but it will have to be considered at some point – there may for example be a trade-off between functionality and price which this evaluation will reveal.

The following questions and points must be rated (each out of 10). Ideally one would have an objective measure, which would stand the test of time and would be applicable in all circumstances. This is not likely to be attainable, and one must settle for the subjective opinion of the evaluator in comparing the particular set of products being considered. This is another reason why it is difficult to use the scores given (for example, in a review of a product) without checking them against one's own experience.

The reason for showing this process in the form of an example applicable to a particular situation is to show the amount of work, ie the number of questions that are likely to be needed for a given organisation. Most of the questions asked in this example will also be applicable in a wider context, though they may need tailoring in some cases. Appendix 2 gives a wide spread of questions which could be included in such an examination – it is however important not to include too many questions for fear of devaluing those which are really important.

Functionality

This set of questions sets out to check whether the product does what is needed in a manner which will be acceptable to the particular people who will be employing it in this organisation – this is another reason why overall judgements of products are not helpful. All this evaluation is to be based on glossy brochures, manuals, demonstrations and information given by salesmen, technical experts and existing users.

1 Ease of set up
The method of setting up files on the system and getting started is rated. Factors considered are the ease of getting from dictionary/directory maintenance to effective use of the system, the clarity of the displays, the general flexibility of the commands and facilities available and the overall power of the language in this area.

2 Ease of screen design
This criterion shows up a number of differences, particularly between products with a screen painter and those without. The former allows the designers to place text and value fields on the screen where they look best; the software converts this to its own table of co-ordinates. This is usually less work than the alternative where the designers have to calculate the co-ordinate positions themselves. The computer software uses these when it needs to draw a screen. There is also a half-way system where the co-ordinates still have to be calculated but the screen is updated at once to show the effect of each additional field. One advantage of having a table of co-ordinates which can be amended is that it can be used as the basis of a system standard, to ensure that a given field always appears in the same position.

3 Validation
A higher score may be given if a wide range of field types is permitted. Some products allow the programmers to specify additional edit patterns to allow them to check complicated codes. It is often vital that there should be some mechanism for checking the contents of code fields against external files or internal tables. It is normally a requirement that range checks can be specified. Other facilities that might influence scores in this area would be the ease of tailoring error messages where required.

4 Logical procedures
It is very important that it should be possible to control the flow

of the system according either to input data or a field within a file or some calculated value. It might be considered vital to be able to control the flow of screens, ie to choose what processing to carry out next.

This can be achieved in various ways: eg using menus, logic statements entered at fixed or specified points in the processing cycle, procedural code (such as IF...THEN constructs), selection of records satisfying certain input criteria, decision tables, etc. All of these work in different ways and which is given the higher marks will depend on the experience and preference of the user organisation and its advisors.

It is not normally satisfactory to be forced to use a high-level language for the purposes of satisfying this requirement.

5 Comprehensive reporting
In order to be considered an application generator and thus to have reached this part of the evaluation process, the product must have reasonable reporting facilities. So higher marks will be given to software for the ease of using these facilities, the level of 'help' available and for the range of reporting options beyond the basics that are to be expected of every product. The ease of amending one report or screen display and all its attributes is also important.

6 Links to other languages
Even though it is always to be hoped that the option will never have to be used, it is nevertheless very useful (particularly for a mature data processing department with existing skills) to be able to carry out any particularly complicated or awkward processing in a high-level language. The particular language chosen will obviously depend on the organisation in question.

7 Immediate execution
One of the most important facets of an application generator which is to be used to improve programmer productivity is that it should be possible to input the control logic and commands interactively from the terminal and immediately execute those commands. A long compilation is found to be less satisfactory, especially where the product is being used in an evolutionary or prototyping mode. Some products offer both an interpreted

mode for development and a compiled mode for greater efficiency of production work. Others only compile individual short modules or programs for which the waiting time is minimal. Choice in this area will depend partly on the need for operational efficiency.

8 Flexibility
If an application generator works on a fixed processing framework or cycle, this can be an inhibiting factor for some processing options. Since no-one can be sure that the systems will all be programmable with a fixed framework, it is very sensible to give higher ratings to languages which are more flexible. It must be pointed out that the simpler system may suit applications with more limited aspirations.

9 Ease of learning
This can be judged from what vendors and existing users say of the length of training required for a programmer to become proficient. This can be cross-checked against the length of training courses offered. It is not possible to get an objective measure for this variable. There is also a need to make sure that short training does not imply a limited functionality.

Files

It should be remembered that in the particular case under discussion it had already been determined that the files should not be held in an internal database format but in the standard manufacturer's file-handling format. Other options were discussed earlier in this chapter and in Chapter 4. The following four additional points are to be taken into account:

1 Availability of files
Where there are other existing systems which are not written in the fourth-generation language, it is a requirement that the files written by the new method should be made available to these other systems. This means low marks for any product which uses its own data compaction routines, even if files could be written in an external format.

2 Access to external files
By the same token it is a requirement that external files should

be available to the application generator. There might be limits on variable length files or any others in a format not specifiable to the directory or dictionary.

3 Relational file capabilities
It is required that the applications should be able to access files in a relational manner, both for the equivalent of 'table-look-up' and also to allow the possibility of updating the related files. It was not thought necessary to have the full power of relational algebra, in the example.

4 File types
To provide the possibility of choice, extra marks are given to products which could deal with both indexed sequential and direct access file organisations. This again gives additional flexibility, particularly when dealing with externally specified files.

Security and Integrity

The following features are considered and rated in this area:

1 Control over file access
It is considered vital that there should be control over access to programs and files. It is not however absolutely essential that this should be automatically provided by the software, so long as it could be easily included in the application design. Obviously higher marks are granted for additional automatic facilities.

2 Field level controls
The ability to control access at field level is seen as very desirable. In some cases this is done by allowing particular groups of people access only to data contained in 'views' to which they are allocated. This means that they never gain access to the real data descriptions behind the views.

3 Data dictionary
Most application generators use their own data directories, and many of them would hardly deserve the name data dictionary. For this reason it is required that there should be a link to a specific (manufacturer supplied) data dictionary, which is to be kept in line automatically with the contents of the files. It is not

necessary that the files should be dynamically created whenever the dictionary is amended. It is interesting that one vendor was able to modify his product to meet this requirement, partly because he had had a number of requests for the same thing. This requirement will vary from organisation to organisation.

4 Logging and recovery
The views of vendors differed significantly as to what could be called satisfactory control over data logging and recovery in the case of breakdown. In some cases everything was automatic, which provided excellent functionality at a cost of processing which was unnecessarily complicated and therefore inefficient for less vital systems. In other cases it was necessary to add a command to write the necessary log file. Any system in which this could not be carried out at all was given no marks in this area.

Efficiency

This proves to be the most difficult area in which to achieve reliable measurement. Very few accurate figures are available. The marking is therefore rather crude and relies on the feelings of people at sites visited and on statements by the vendors' representatives. It can of course be checked at the stage where trials are carried out.

1 Use of machine resources
How important this is to a given installation will depend on the loading on the computer being considered. It may be unimportant or of the utmost significance.

2 File usage
The efficiency of storage is desirable in order to reduce costs overall. It may be more important to keep file access times small in order to speed up the processing of large files in particular.

3 Response times
The only problem encountered in this area concerns the use of large amounts of data which caused problems in at least one case. This point is easy to check out initially in demonstrations and later with something approaching the real mix of jobs on one's own computer system, even if the actual loading has to be simulated.

Support

Documentation, training and field support should all be considered. Training courses should be available for basic training in the application generator and it is to be seen as a bonus if advanced programming courses or courses in design are also available. It will be acceptable for an initial course to be available on the purchaser's site but this may not be convenient for subsequent training where fewer people may require a course at the same time. For this reason public courses may be preferable. On support, the geographical positioning of support services will be seen as important, as well as the availability of 'on-site' assistance and telephone advice, both from the vendor and, if necessary, the actual developer of the software.

Reputation

The standing and reputation of the supplier of the software and of the product and its authors must also be considered carefully. The number of existing customers (on the right hardware) is also important, and should be considered alongside the number of support staff who are going to be supporting the product, as discovered under the previous heading.

Portability

The ease of transferring onto another computer manufacturer's hardware may also be of interest – particularly where, for example, a version of the software is available on personal computers. This will probably be rated quite low by most installations, unless they already operate in a mixed environment or envisage the possible or planned need for a migration path.

Price

How important is price? Each organisation must decide for itself whether it will be willing to pay more to gain more functionality. Perhaps it will come to its decision on technical grounds and use the price check mainly to decide between otherwise equal products. The danger of this approach is perhaps that the more expensive products will be better and may have more functions than are really required. One could therefore deliberately include, on the shortlist, products at different points on the price scale.

Ideally too one should attempt an assessment of cost beyond merely the consideration of price alone. One might well include the cost of maintenance over perhaps five years, the cost of training and support and the vendor's policy over the supply of updates.

If it is likely that more than one copy of the software will be required for other computers on the same site, as is not uncommon with large organisations using minicomputers, the price check should look at the discount policy of the vendor for the number of copies likely to be required; it may be that the more expensive software becomes cheaper when multiple copies are purchased.

Result of Evaluation

An example is given below of the result of such an evaluation. Table 5.1 shows the raw scores for the questions and the accumulation to group totals, while Table 5.2 contains the adjusted totals.

It is interesting to study the hypothetical example given here. It might seem from a study of the raw scores alone that Product A is the clear leader. The adjustments however change the position to allow Product C almost to catch up. It can then give rise to a debate about whether 'file handling' and 'portability' outweigh 'security' and 'price'.

Since however the evaluation can be used to select products for further trials, it may be that both products will be further evaluated, as described below.

	PRODUCTS		
	A	B	C
Functional Scope			
Set up	5	10	7
Screen design	7	5	10
Validation	9	8	7
Logic	10	5	8
Reporting	8	10	8
Language interface	10	2	9
Immediate execution	10	10	10
Flexibility	8	6	8
Ease of learning	7	10	7
Sub-total	74	66	74

	PRODUCTS		
	A	B	C
Carried forward	74	66	74
Files			
Files available	10	3	10
Access to external files	10	10	10
Relational capabilities	6	8	5
File types	10	5	5
Sub-total	36	26	30
Security			
Controlled access	10	10	10
Field access	5	3	8
Data dictionary	3	5	10
Recovery	4	8	6
Sub-total	22	26	34
Efficiency			
Computer resources	6	10	8
Files	10	10	8
Response times	7	5	7
Sub-total	23	25	23
Support			
Documentation	5	7	4
Training	10	8	6
Field support	9	5	7
Sub-total	24	20	17
Reputation			
Supplier	7	7	6
Product	8	9	4
Authors	6	6	7
No of customers	7	10	5
Sub-total	28	32	22
Portability			
Other mainframes	5	10	0
Personal computers	10	0	0
Sub-total	15	10	0
Price			
Basic	2	6	10
Multiple copies	4	6	6
Sub-total	6	12	16
UNADJUSTED TOTALS	228	217	216

Table 5.1 Evaluation of Application Generators – Unadjusted

ADJUSTED SUB-TOTAL SCORES

	maximum	PRODUCTS A	B	C
Functional scope	30	24.7	22	24.7
Files	20	18	13	15
Security	20	11	13	17
Efficiency	10	7.7	8.3	7.7
Support	5	4	3.3	2.8
Reputation	5	3.5	4	2.7
Portability	5	3.7	2.5	0
Price	5	1.5	3	4
ADJUSTED TOTALS		74.1	69.2	73.9

Table 5.2 Evaluation of Application Generators - Adjusted

Note that the adjusted score is calculated by taking the unadjusted figure, multiplying it by the relevant contribution value and dividing it by the maximum raw score for the section. If there are nine questions the maximum unadjusted score is 90. To give an adjusted maximum of 30, one therefore multiplies by 30 and then divides by 90.

TRIALS OF SHORTLISTED PRODUCTS

Wherever possible a trial should be carried out on one or more products. If there is one clear leader at this stage, this product may be selected alone. It is perhaps more likely that there will be doubts about the best product and for this reason a closer examination is advisable. Trials will clearly provide more information about the products and thus aid the final selection process.

To be useful in this context a trial must:

— produce a system, however small, that the organisation selecting can recognise as being useful. A standard benchmark will not have the same effect;

— produce this in a limited timescale. Where two or more products are involved, the time, facilities and environment must be the same in all cases. A trial lasting one or two days is suggested;

— be carried out on the premises of the purchaser in order to control the time and effort spent;

— be produced by a programmer (or designer or analyst) of approximately equal experience. Assuming that no in-house experience is available, the personnel involved may be provided by the vendor or a systems house.

Another option is to see what can be produced by one's own staff, in say a week or two, but this may run into learning problems which have in themselves nothing to do with the capabilities of the language.

The purpose of such a trial will be to test out a number of features of the products. It will never be possible to test out all the features of an application generator in such a brief trial, but it is certain that a great deal of value can be learned from the way the trial problem is approached by the programmer, as well as from discovery of what a given product cannot do.

It is often found that the sight of a meaningful application, however small, tackled and completed 'in-house' will open minds both of data processing staff and of potential users. It will also offer the possibility of a more detailed examination of critical features.

It is easier, since only two products at most are now involved, to reconsider those areas where there were differences. One can in effect widen the scales, since a direct comparison will normally reveal that one application generator is more appropriate than the other. It is interesting that one organisation shortlisted two products and could hardly differentiate between them. Yet after more detailed tests and more exposure to both, one of the two became the clear winner on all but one of the evaluation criteria.

OTHER MEANS OF SELECTION

The trials should be supplemented by visits to existing users. The vendor will usually be able to suggest reference sites, but it can be very valuable to visit organisations selected by other means if possible. (These visits may have been carried out at the earlier stages by the evaluator, but it may be possible to take a larger team including one or more users, especially if the installation visited is carrying out projects in the same area.) One organisation involved a wide spectrum of people (including DP management, technical and operations staff as well as a sprinkling of knowledgeable users) in half-day seminars at which vendors would make a full presentation of their products. All these people were then allowed to 'vote' on different aspects of the application generators that they had seen. It is of course important that end-users are included in the selection of products for end-users. From this process two clear favourites emerged, one of which was chosen on technical grounds after a further examination. In the event the final choice was swayed by the presence of certain facilities in one of these two products that were only promised in the other (at a different date the choice might have been different). It is interesting that the final technical comparison made the chosen software product appear much better than the other, even though in the earlier stages they had been neck and neck. When only two products have to be compared, it is worth looking closely to find even minor differences.

SELECTING THE INITIAL APPLICATIONS

When an application generator has been chosen, it should still be regarded as under trial for at least its first application. It will have many features that can only be revealed in use: it will be important to see how systems behave in a live environment with an existing load of other work and with large volumes of data. Input from real users can bring some surprises too. The contract should therefore make it clear that there are performance requirements still to be satisfied. Tests of these matters should be planned rather than haphazard – it may even be possible to complete all necessary tests during a 'free trial' period of a month or even longer, which will itself need careful planning.

This leads to consideration of whether programming of such initial applications should be carried out by 'experts' employed by the vendor or an external software house, or by the staff of the organisation purchasing the software. The latter would probably be coming into contact with the language for the first time and would not be familiar with it. The balance between these two positions is quite difficult to find, for the following reasons:

- if design and programming is performed by outside experts, it is probable that better results will be gained at least in the short term;

— in-house staff have to learn sometime and may therefore benefit from exposure to the product as soon as it can be arranged;

— a compromise that might be considered is to make as much use of one's own staff as possible, but to employ the vendors to provide consultancy advice particularly on design aspects where a novice might fall into a number of traps.

Before any programming is done, it is recommended that proper data analysis be carried out. This will make sure that files or database are able to respond efficiently to the updating and enquiries and reports that will be required of the system. The use of a structured methodology such as SSADM (Structured Systems Analysis and Design Method) which employs formal or semi-formal data analysis techniques will do much to minimise problems in this area.

To evaluate the results of such a 'trial' application one must assess it (a) in terms of the tests specified in the contract and (b) by looking at all the features and facets considered in the 'paper' evaluation to see if the use of the product has given rise to any change of view on any of the scores. It is worth saying that even if one has to re-assess the scores, this does not necessarily change its position relative to alternative products with which one has not had practical experience. One must however admit the possibility that the wrong choice has been made. In one organisation it was only when a test involving realistic volumes of data was carried out that the response times showed themselves to be quite unacceptable. There are also cases where it was quite clear, in well under a month, that the new way of working was indeed very attractive, so that there was, in the words of one analyst/programmer, "no way that we would allow it to be taken away, if we can help it".

COMPLETION OF EVALUATION

It may be assumed that the evaluation process is completed when a firm decision has been made about whether to purchase and use the product. It is at this point that one must make sure that one takes (or has taken) the right organisational decisions to accompany one's use of the fourth-generation tool. This topic is described in Chapter 6.

6 Effective Use of Application Generation Tools

CHANGES NEEDED TO ORGANISATION

The organisation and method of working of the computer department may have to be changed to accommodate the new tools. It is worth looking at how some data processing departments using them have evolved. This chapter considers such aspects as policy, management, staffing, training and standards.

An overview is also given to appropriate changes in development methods. In particular, a brief introduction is given to the effects of fourth-generation languages on the development life-cycle.

It has been said that it is easier to introduce an application generator into a 'green field' site than into an existing installation, because of the resistance from programmers who are used to COBOL and other procedural languages. There are however sufficient instances where this is not the case (ie where application generators have been successfully introduced into existing sites) to make it worthwhile looking for the reasons. In general it will be found that a good overall strategy and approach to change can provide the answer.

OVERALL POLICY

Every organisation purchasing application generators should define what its policies are for their use. Clearly these policies must differ according to the needs of the organisation, and it is as well to realise how much these can differ. This is by way of a warning to readers to make sure that they only implement organisation changes which are truly applicable to their own situation.

Whereas one organisation might decide that the new development tools will be used for all new applications, except where they have been proved to be unsuitable, another might prefer to use them only for the provision of query facilities to user departments.

The following points were included in one organisation's Software Policy document:

— From now on, all application development must be carried out using PRODUCT A. This covers the full range of development services from small-scale to large-scale systems development. The product will also be tried out as a development tool by some selected users;

— As now, package-based solutions will continue to be evaluated alongside 'in-house' solutions;

— The new policy means that development using PL/1, CICS, DMS, GIS, VSPC, etc will be phased out. Not only new systems but also enhancements to existing systems, *wherever possible,* must be done using PRODUCT A. Any exceptions from this policy must be clearly justified in writing when the proposal is prepared;

— We will continue, of course, to support existing facilities because we have 74 operational systems written using them. We will aim however to phase out some facilities (eg GIS, ADRS, ADI after two years);

— Our pilot schemes using the new product point to a halving of development costs/timescales for typical projects; some phases in fact will see greater improvements than this while others remain the same. There will be an increase in machine resource usage which will be compensated for by a reduction in the unit rates with a replacement mainframe computer during 1985. The net result will be that in general running costs will remain approximately the same;

— PRODUCT A should enable us to replace some of our older systems much more quickly and effectively. This will be a part of the new policy actively pursued by the Systems Development Section. Every opportunity should be taken to replace parts or all of existing facilities by the new product in the older systems;

- We will also see that using PRODUCT A will lead to a radical change in our methodology. For example:
  - much more emphasis on prototypes being developed leading to the final solutions;
  - much less technical documentation;
  - much more involvement from users in the crucial early phase of development;
  - much more orientation by our staff to user needs (but we will very much need a nucleus of technical experts);
- It is intended to set up some informal group which should monitor the growth in the use of PRODUCT A, identifying technical problems, proposing ways round these problems and recording the good and bad features of the product so that a working set of guidelines can be developed and experience shared;
- We are arranging training for all appropriate staff;
- Please ensure that all your staff see this note. This should be an exciting step forward for everyone concerned and enable us to provide a big improvement in our services.

These statements need only slight amplification to enable the context to be understood. The organisation in question did not plan to use the application generator for its major transaction-based systems which were already running satisfactorily using a package. The rest of the work was for a wide range of departments, none of which had 'volume' problems. The original impetus behind the decision to buy a fourth-generation language was to get rid of a backlog of work – in the event they found that the use of the product found a quite different backlog of small- to medium-sized systems which the user departments wanted but had never requested before because of the known backlog.

The publication of this policy document followed a very thorough evaluation of those languages which were suitable for this task. It is significant that in the two years between the issuing of this document and the publication of this book the executive who issued the document saw no reason to withdraw the statements.

This document itself, signed by the DP Director, is evidence of high-level commitment which all organisations are recommended to copy.

STAFFING

There are a number of different ways of organising staff where application generators are to be used. Not all organisations have changed from the traditional structure with teams of analysts and programmers. There is however a noticeable trend towards a reduction in team size and the use of analyst/programmers rather than keeping the roles separate.

Some of the greatest productivity gains have been found where all design and programming is carried out by experienced analyst/programmers working for the most part on their own, or at most in small teams. The advantages include a reduced (if not eliminated) need for the passing of specifications from one person to another. This gives a clear gain both in time and accuracy. Because experienced staff are used, there is less likelihood of mistakes, and one-person teams imply a single point of contact for users. The following problems may sometimes be found with this form of organisation:

- it does nothing to train people to take over if a key member of staff leaves;
- one may in effect employ too highly skilled personnel on tasks which could be delegated;
- because only one person is engaged on a given project it may prove harder to organise 'walkthroughs' and to ensure that documentation is complete: this could be overcome by keeping a second person up-to-date on each project. Documentation will be necessary for this purpose, which 'one man' teams are not always very motivated to provide because they have, 'in their head', all the knowledge they need.

Another approach to the staffing structure is to set up small teams of two, three or four people where the senior partner organises the work of the juniors and is otherwise free to act as contact point for the users and to carry out the more difficult design and programming tasks. A team of three can be convenient for the arrangement of 'walkthroughs' as everyone in the team can keep sufficiently up-to-date on all the programs. This will also provide back-up in the case of people leaving the team, especially if there is proper documentation.

It is interesting to find that one organisation with larger teams of about seven staff, equivalent in size to the teams they were used to previously, found that, although the term 'analyst/programmer' was used at all levels, senior people still tended to carry out analysis and user-liaison functions, leaving most of the programming to the more junior staff.

Considerable reductions in staff numbers can be achieved, if required. It is important to decide whether productivity improvement should mean producing the same systems with fewer people or producing enhanced systems with as many people as are needed to product them. A very modest saving in staff numbers, or even no decrease at all, may prove to be the most effective policy.

It is sometimes found that programmers who are very experienced in COBOL, PL/1 and similar languages find some difficulty in adapting to the new environment. This is partly because they are used to thinking in procedural language terms and partly that they find less of a challenge in using labour-reducing tools to produce systems. The answer may lie in presenting the real purpose of the data processing function to them effectively when the tools are introduced, suggesting that there is quite as much challenge in getting users to specify and accept new systems. In fact organisations have usually managed to overcome the objections of programming staff and to obtain a high level of involvement.

USER INVOLVEMENT

The involvement of users in the production of systems should be carefully considered. This is different from merely involving them in design decisions, which is becoming accepted as an improved approach. If too much of the process of design and programming is pushed onto them, this may be a counter-productive use of manpower. If all that is happening is that the programming is being moved from a separate data processing department into the user area, this is not productive unless advantages accrue – perhaps from closer proximity to the potential end-users or by the fact that someone who has done a given job is involved in its conversion to a computer system (even here he may lose some effectiveness as an end-user). Nevertheless many organisations have welcomed such involvement, particularly in setting up enquiries and reports. Given a report generator or query language as part of the application generator which is easy to use, there is no reason why users should not write many of their own reports and queries.

This means that they must understand the structure of the stored data. Worries have been expressed about whether the data will always be properly understood and that people might draw unjustified conclusions from it. This is perhaps a reflection on the DP department if they are not able to explain what is actually in the data files, and perhaps the database structure has been made complicated for reasons of computer efficiency. Proper data analysis and the explanation of the results to the users will help.

This is one reason why it is useful to provide extracted files containing the information required by user departments for reports, etc, rather than allowing them to access operational files. This also makes it less likely that they will make use of very inefficient file searches, which can happen if one allows people unrestricted access to the main data files. Products which allow the end-user to be restricted to a more limited 'view' of the data files will help here.

MANAGEMENT

No particular changes in management style have been reported. During the changeover period to the new tools, control needs to be maintained. Perhaps programmers will exhibit signs of lowered morale if they perceive that their skills are not so much in demand. This must be countered by making people realise how valuable their work is to the organisation. In fact good user reaction to the systems produced by the application generator tools will almost inevitably lead to an improvement in morale within the DP department. Changes in the ways of working as outlined above will lead to some changes of role – chief programmers may be less needed as such but might find themselves working in much more of an advisory or consultancy role, with some responsibility for training both DP and user staff.

Closer links with the user community can lead to the formation of teams associated directly with particular functions within the company, even with physical siting within the user section. This sort of change is only indirectly caused by the introduction of application generators but it has been one of the by-products in some companies, partly because the users have found themselves more involved with the design of the system. If this were to lead to a complete fragmentation of the data processing function, this might lead to less effective use of the talent available: one 'functional' section might become overmanned at the expense of another. Fortunately this effect is not common.

THE DEVELOPMENT LIFE-CYCLE

The traditional development process can be described in terms of a life-cycle with the following stages:

- initiation;
- analysis;
- design;
- programming;
- unit testing;
- integration testing;
- systems acceptance;
- operation;
- maintenance.

Using application generators there may need to be some changes to this. The larger the development, the fewer the changes. For example, in a development requiring several man-years, one would expect to see some blurring of the strict distinction between analysis, design and programming, because some of the functions normally carried out separately will be performed by the same person.

The use of prototyping or evolutionary development will make some differences to this life-cycle, which would then look more like this:

— initiation;
— first-stage analysis;
— design and programming of prototype;
— review;
— amend as necessary;
— design and programming of final system;
— test;
— integration test;
— systems acceptance test;
— operation.

Within this cycle of the life of a project one may in fact repeat the prototyping as often as necessary.

For smaller systems, a much simpler life-cycle model will be sufficient:

— initiation;
— problem and data analysis;
— design and programming;
— testing;
— acceptance;
— operation.

Where carried out by one-person teams, indeed even the distinction between analysis and design might disappear in practice, but the function remains even if there is not really a separate phase.

TRAINING

It will be necessary to provide different levels of training for different people, such as:

— designers of major systems;
— developers of major systems;

— developers of simpler systems;

— users needing instruction on the report generator;

— users requiring to understand more about the concepts so that they can take part more effectively in the design process.

It must therefore be discovered whether these differences are catered for by the range of courses offered by the vendor (or in some cases by independent training or software houses). Often a basic course, perhaps of one week's duration, will be available. More advanced courses including assistance on systems design aspects are not so common. (This might then be one of the criteria by which one judges 'training' during the evaluation process.) Another way of acquiring this kind of knowledge would be to make use of the support staff – as described below; this is more likely to succeed in a small department where there are not too many people requiring assistance in the early stages and the advice would not become too diluted.

Users may be satisfied with a one-day course covering selected features and probably run by the data processing department. It is useful to make this an in-house course even if the initial courses have to be provided by outside sources due to a lack of internal experts; this is because users need to know about the data as well as just the language features. Applied training will therefore be of more use to the users. Some products prompt their users by giving them a list of fields available to the request from which to make their selection; this can only work if the users understand the data.

DOCUMENTATION

There is a certain level of documentation that one can reasonably demand from software such as application generators. If the product is self-explanatory in use it is possible to make do with the minimum of documentary assistance.

A 'reference manual' should always be expected. This will be a comprehensive document giving details of all options that can be chosen – and, just as important, all error messages that can occur. This leaves as an area to be decided by the writers of the reference document whether they need to include any operating system commands and messages, but ideally the application generation environment should for the most part protect its users from the operating system so that this conflict will not arise.

If the reference manual does not contain examples of the use of particular features (probably for reasons of not making the document too large and unwieldy), a 'training' or 'user' manual will be a useful addition to the documentation. The authors or vendors of software products sometimes provide an 'introductory' manual which is a simplified version of the comprehensive user manual. This can be a very useful feature, particularly for new users of the product or as a reminder for those who only use it irregularly. It is beneficial to be able to have on-line self-help tutorial material for use by students on an individual basis. A reference card including a guide to function and control keys can be of value.

One very useful feature is to have on-line reference material in the form of 'help' screens explaining how to carry out the various operations. It is particularly helpful if these are 'context related' – ie relevant to the use of the command in the present situation if there is any possible confusion. They should also be at varying levels of detail to suit, at the highest level, those who need only a quick reminder but giving more detail to those who need a fuller explanation. Such 'help' messages should also be built into systems for the end-user – this is relevant here because it is a feature of some fourth-generation languages that they provide the skeleton processing to allow the application programmer the facility of achieving this aim very easily. It is also beneficial if all these messages and screens can be amended by the user organisation. There are certain occasions where this is particularly useful:

- where a system is likely to be used in more than one country; by, for example, a multinational company;

- where words that have a particular local meaning are used in a different context within the 'help' screens. This is liable to cause confusion which could have been avoided;

- to allow the messages to be tailored by the purchaser into a standard pattern or format in order to bring it into line with other systems with which the potential users are already familiar.

SUPPORT

It is important that the maximum use is made of any support offered by the vendors. This must be used to improve the standard of knowledge of one's own staff. Thus if a certain number of days are offered free, they should certainly be used – but not all at once when the product is installed. Some days of support should be kept in hand until one's own staff have gained the basic knowledge about the software and are therefore able to reap the benefit of more advanced advice. (This may be a counsel of perfection – but if the free advice is all used up in the early stages it would be sensible to budget for the hire of support later on, especially if advanced courses are not available.) Support personnel on-site can look at one's actual applications and get involved in the solution of real problems.

Some vendors offer the facility of a telephone 'help-line'. It is important that as far as possible the technical contact with the vendor should be channelled through the same person at the purchaser's end. The purpose is to protect the vendor from problems that could be solved locally and to ensure that one person knows of all the problems that have arisen in case of further occurrences of the same problem. This has its implications on the organisation of the data processing department, since someone must be given the responsibility and the time to carry out this role. There may be geographical or organisational reasons why a single contact cannot be arranged and in this case the minimum possible number of staff should be authorised to use the 'help-line'. It is not to be expected that a 'help-line' service will be available out of normal working hours and this would be expensive to organise. Occasionally there is a point of contact in the USA which could be used in the evenings at the cost of an international telephone call.

Internal support might take the form of an internal 'help-line' within the DP department, in the information centre if there is one. The organisation of this can be as formal or informal as is desired. If there are a lot of users in a particular department, it can be worth ensuring, for all the reasons described above, that one of them becomes the local point of contact.

STANDARDS

A balance is required between the use of very elaborate (and hence expensive) standards and the confusion that can arise if there are none at all. It is believed that the standards necessary for the employment of fourth-generation languages should be simpler than those that are required in more traditional development environments; this is because the language itself will impose some standards of its own. This section can be no more than an introduction to areas where standards should be considered. Many of the things that need to be done are product specific and must therefore be discussed with the supplier or existing users of the language. The user group could be useful as a point of contact; many products are backed up by a group of this sort.

The most important areas to consider are those concerning the security of programs and data. These are discussed separately.

Program Security and other Standards

There will always be critical systems such as those which update files containing sensitive production, financial or personal data. It is therefore stressed that proper control should be maintained over the programs which carry out these functions. It may be advantageous to keep these programs in one or more production libraries to which changes can only be made under controlled procedures. This can be organised so as to prevent unauthorised amendments by using any facilities provided with the application generator or the system software to give updating only to persons properly authorised. There are language systems which provide utilities to facilitate the transfer of programs from development to production libraries.

Another very useful facility is to be able to see where (and when) amendments have been carried out. Some installations have even written their own routines to list the latest date against every line of code changed. (It will not however take note of deletions unless specific comments are written.) Even where automatic updating is not possible it may be possible to indicate in comments where amendments have been made. This also indicates the need for proper logging of all amendments to production programs as with any other language. This is probably made easier by the fact that in general programs are much shorter.

As with most languages it will be possible to make the coding clearer by the use of spacing, comments, indentation, etc. With report specifications that can be written in an extended string it will be worth limiting the number of parameters per line.

The need for conventions concerning program and field names is no different from the position in a traditional data processing department. If the programs are held within a private library it probably does not matter too much but with any shared data control is essential. It is not helpful to have several programs all called 'UPDATE'.

Data Security and Standards

Many of the comments about program security and standards apply equally to data. Whether large or small numbers of people have access to files for enquiry purposes, with a language which allows them to generate their own reports and enquiries, it is clearly vital only to allow them access to data for which they have authorisation. This can either be done by providing files of data specially set up with only the authorised data or by making use of any facilities for control of access down to field level, in some cases by developing a 'view' of the data which is available to users with a particular profile.

It is advisable to have an installation-wide standard on file and field names to avoid all confusion. There is a problem that people making enquiries probably react better to a field called PRODUCT than to one called PX2PROD – if names of this type have to be used, the reasons will have to be explained to users. Languages which limit field names to eight characters or less suffer most from problems of coded and meaningless field names.

Audit Trails

Another facet of security that needs to be addressed is that adequate audit trails may need to be provided. It will therefore be necessary to satisfy both external and internal auditors that the controls that have been put into the system are to their satisfaction. This is no problem where all updating is under the direct control of the programmer, since the audit trail information can be written just as it would have been in a COBOL system, either on the master file or on a subsidiary audit file. Where however the application generator takes care of all updating without the need for specific file handling commands, through its internal structure or framework, it may be more difficult to persuade the auditors that audit trail information held on the master file is fully under the control of the programmer and in this case a separate audit file would be a better solution. If this is the path chosen, it is also necessary to consider whether it is possible for the two files to get out of step. If it is not possible to find an adequate solution then perhaps the wrong product has been chosen. This should be one of the factors considered during the evaluation process.

CONTROL OVER SYSTEM USAGE

One of the effects of introducing an application generator which permits on-line ad-hoc enquiries or the development of personal systems by end-users is undoubtedly a growth in systems; more often than not, it seems that this growth is greater than had been anticipated. This is rightly seen as a potential threat, in that the unplanned growth will eventually lead to a real crisis as the need for additional hardware, disk storage, etc arises.

Organisations need to come to terms with this. Prevention is perhaps only possible by not allowing the use of the tools at all, but control can be attempted by price policies and by strict supervision of all usage of computing and disk resources. The assumption must be that if the users want to spend their budgets on their on-line systems they have the right to do so. If this means that the computer installation will have to expand, that is the right thing to happen. Those who have reported this phenomenon have also noted that the fact that hardware prices have been falling at the same time means that the unplanned growth does not actually cost as much as might have been feared.

There is then still a need for some control to be exercised over programs and data being held on the system but not utilised. After a certain period, which will vary from installation to installation, it may be possible to archive unused data if there has been no specific request to keep it on-line for future use. This should only be necessary in the case of 'non-standard' or personal data, as the parameters for the retention of data from regular systems should have been agreed during their development.

SUMMARY

The application generator has settled down and is going through a period of consolidation. Products now on the market are much more robust and worthwhile than was the case a few years ago.

Sensible DP managers will recognise the productivity gains that are there to be made. The aim should be to adopt those tools which will give productivity in the true sense of improving the information flow within the organisation – and thus improving profits. They will not expect to see startling advances in the near future and should therefore look now for the tools which meet their organisation's real needs.

Looking further ahead, it is likely that there will be greater integration of all information and decision support functions. There will be better links to the diagramming tools used in the analysis phase of the life-cycle. It is further to be expected that the best of today's tools will have survived and will be available for the analyst and programmer in versions which run on workstations on their own desks with links to each other in a distributed environment. Now is the right time to get to know how to develop systems using application generators in the ways explored in this book.

Appendix 1
Evaluation Criteria

This appendix lists the evaluation criteria discussed in Chapter 5. It must not be forgotten that this is based on the requirements of a real organisation. This gives a much better picture of the level of questions that need to be asked for a single evaluation than a generalised list, of which there follows an example in Appendix 2; some of the questions are of such minor importance that their presence in the list would obscure the differences between products under evaluation.

The other important consideration is that the percentage figures given to the various headings must be considered afresh for each new evaluation. The weightings show a reasonable balance, given the number of questions asked in each category. Adding more questions reduces the value of each question.

1 Functionality

- How easy is it to set up systems?
- Is screen design easy?
- Does it allow a wide range of validation methods, including range checking and table-look-up?
- Does it give the ability to carry out logical processing?
- Are the reporting capabilities comprehensive?
- Does it have the means of linking to other languages?
- Is it quick to use, giving immediate execution after anything has been changed?

— Is it flexible or does it force one to follow the fixed framework?

— Does it give the ability to 'navigate' from screen to screen without recourse to a main menu?

2 Files

— Are all files available to other users where necessary?

— Are files ISAM (or direct access)?

— Does the product have relational file handling?

— Can it access files from other systems?

3 Security

— Is there security over file access?

— Is there any control at field level?

— Does the product have its own data dictionary? Are there links to any proprietary data dictionaries?

— Is there adequate control over logging and recovery?

4 Efficiency

— Is the application generator efficient in its use of computer memory and processor time?

— Is it efficient in its use of files?

— Will it give an acceptable response time?

5 Support

— Is documentation adequate?

— Is training available?

— Is support likely to be provided well?

6 Reputation (of both Product and Vendor)

— What are people saying about the product? Is it properly tested?

— How many have been sold in the UK and worldwide?

— Is the firm selling and supporting the product of good standing?

— Do they use the product themselves?

— How helpful have they been during the evaluation?

— Are they good at demonstrating the product?

— Is their geographical location satisfactory?

7 Portability

— Can the product be used on other hardware?

— In particular, is there a microcomputer version?

8 Price

— The total cost of the software is taken into account – the lowest cost receives the highest score. Note: if more than one copy of the software is required there may be quantity discounts available.

Appendix 2
Product Survey Questionnaire

This appendix contains the comprehensive questionnaire used by CCTA (the Central Computer and Telecommunications Agency) of HM Treasury in a survey of application generators.

It will be found to be too detailed to be used in the direct comparison of products, especially in the earlier stages of the evaluation, without considerable effort in deciding which questions are of real importance to the particular organisation.

It should therefore be used as a checklist against which the selected product can be compared to ensure that it has no vital parts missing. It may equally be used wherever the differences between products are such that the evaluation has become very difficult – a more detailed checklist can be of use in such a situation.

SECTION A – SUMMARY

Name of Product:

Current release level:

Product Description: A brief description of the product and its capabilities

SECTION B - ADMINISTRATION RECORD

Completed by ....

Company/Department ....

Date ....

Checked by ....

Company/Department ....

Date ....

SECTION C - GENERAL INFORMATION

1. Supplier Information

1.1 Name, address and telephone number of vendor.

1.2 Name and telephone number of person(s) to contact for further details, if necessary, regarding

1.2.1 Marketing information.

1.2.2 Technical support.

1.3 How long has the company been in operation

1.3.1 in the UK?

1.3.2 world-wide?

1.4 Was the product originally developed by the above vendor?

2. Product History

2.1 When was the product first installed at a customer site for customer usage?

2.2 How frequently do major product releases occur? When was the last major release and when is the next one planned?

2.3 What enhancements, if any, are planned for the product and when will they be introduced?

3. Users of Product

3.1 How many users of the product are there

3.1.1 in the UK?

3.1.1.1 within Government?

3.1.1.2 outside Government?

3.1.2 elsewhere in Europe?

3.1.3 elsewhere?

3.2 Describe any previous projects using this product with which the company has been involved both inside and outside of Government. Please indicate the size and complexity of the jobs in broad terms.

3.3 Please give the name and address of a reference site which we may contact if necessary.

3.4 Is there an active user group in the UK? If so, plcase give name, address and telephone number of a contact.

3.5 Who are expected to be the principal users of the product

3.5.1 non-DP staff?

3.5.2 analysts?

3.5.3 novice programmers?

3.5.4 experienced programmers?

3.5.5 others (please specify)?

SECTION D – TECHNICAL INFORMATION

1. Product Development Status

1.1 What is the current development stage of the product?

(a) static

(b) functionally stable but being cosmetically enhanced

(c) being functionally enhanced

(d) being migrated onto other machine environments

2. Operating Environment: Application Generator

2.1 On what machine/operating system/TP monitor combinations does the product run?

2.2 Do any components of the product require a batch environment? If so, which?

2.3 Can those components of the product which are normally used in a TP environment also operate in a batch environment?

2.4 What is the main storage requirement for the application generator

2.4.1 when operating on-line?

2.4.2 when operating in batch?

2.5 Is it necessary to incorporate any non-standard features within the operating system or the TP monitor to support the application generator?

2.6 Are there any other software components not previously mentioned (from any vendor source) which are required when developing applications?

3. Operating Environment: Application

3.1 On what machine/operating system/TP monitor combinations can the generated application run?

3.2 Are TP applications supported? If so, what is the main storage requirement of the on-line run-time system?

3.3 Are batch applications supported? If so, what is the main storage requirement of the batch run-time system?

3.4 Can a TP application be operated in batch mode?

3.5 Are any cross-machine or cross-software-environment generator versions of the product available? If so, which combinations are supported?

3.6 Are there any other software components not previously mentioned (from any vendor source) which are required when running the generated application?

4. Application Specification Maintenance

4.1 How is the application specification stored?

(a) host operating system file

(b) conventional database file

(c) host operating system library file

(d) application generator's own file system

(e) application generator's own data dictionary system

(f) proprietary data dictionary system (please specify)

(g) other (please specify)

4.2 If the application specification is not stored within a conventional proprietary data dictionary, is bridging software available to relate the application specification to a proprietary data dictionary? If so, which dictionaries and how?

4.3 How is the application specification maintained?

(a) host operating system file editor

(b) data dictionary editor

(c) application generator's own editor(s)

(d) other (please specify)

4.4 Is the editor used to maintain the application specification

(a) line based?

(b) context based?

(c) 'full screen' based?

(d) based on the use of formatted screens?

4.5 Does the generator allow the definition of separate individual user and production application specification libraries?

4.5.1 How can these libraries be protected from unauthorised use?

4.6 What information is logged when an application specification

4.6.1 has the source accessed?

4.6.2 has the source amended?

4.6.3 is re-compiled into an application program?

4.7 Does the application generator provide accounting information to enable the costing of application specification maintenance and development?

5. Application Specification Language

5.1 Because of the variety of approaches adopted for specifying applications, please provide short annotated examples of actual applications. Examples taken from training manuals will usually be satisfactory.

5.2 Is the same language used to specify both batch and on-line applications?

5.3 If the application generator operates on a range of machines or under a range of operating and TP systems, to what extent are application specifications portable across these machines and environments?

5.4 Is it normal to write the entire application in the generator's application specification language, or is it usual to use a conventional programming language for parts of the application?

5.5 Is it possible to specify the invocation of subroutines or procedures written in a conventional programming language from within an application? If so, which languages are supported?

6. Application Architecture: On-Line Applications

6.1 What is the relationship between the host TP system's transactions and the generated application's exchanges (screens)? For example, does an entire generated TP application execute as a single host system conversational transaction?

6.2 To use a generated on-line application, does the user

(a) invoke the same log-on sequence as used by the generator when specifying an application?

(b) invoke a log-on sequence designed as part of the application?

(c) use the TP monitor's standard log-on sequence?

(d) other? (please specify)

6.3 What is the control mechanism to move from one exchange (screen) to the next?

(a) the user specifies the transaction code of the next exchange (screen) explicitly

(b) the user is automatically returned to a central menu where he specifically selects the next exchange

(c) the application decides based upon the user's input

6.4 From one exchange (screen), can the application

6.4.1 access more than one record (segment) of a particular type?

6.4.2 update, create, or delete more than one record (segment) of a particular type?

6.4.3 access more than one type of record?

6.4.4 update, create or delete occurrences of records of different types?

6.5 Can data be passed from one exchange to another? If so, what are the restrictions on its size and format? Is the size and format under the control of the application specification or is it a system default?

6.6 Is the area used to pass data between exchanges recoverable in the event of a system failure?

6.7 Can reports be produced on the line printer from within an on-line application?

7. Application Architecture: Batch Applications

7.1 Can a batch application

7.1.1 update databases or files?

7.1.2 produce reports on a printer from databases or files?

7.2 How are batch applications initiated?

(a) via job control

(b) from within a generated on-line application

(c) from a host TP system transaction

7.3 Can a batch application

7.3.1 access more than one record (segment) of a particular type?

7.3.2 update, create or delete more than one occurrence of a record (segment) of a particular type?

7.3.3 access more than one type of record (segment)?

7.3.4 update, create or delete occurrences of records of different types?

7.4 Can batch and on-line applications have concurrent access to the same databases (files)? If so, what facilities are provided to control concurrent access and maintain data integrity?

7.5 Do batch applications run as independent programs or do they execute under some form of application generator run-time control routine?

8A Source Language Generator Systems

(Use this section if the application generator produces conventional source code as a step in the application development, otherwise use Section 8B.)

8.1 What languages can be generated?

8.2 Does the generator operate as a batch or pseudo-batch job?

8.3 How is the generator invoked?

- (a) directly from the application specification maintenance subsystem
- (b) using job control

8.4 Is the generated code well structured?

8.5 Are meaningful data names used?

8.6 Is any documentation also generated? If so, what?

8.7 What is the smallest component of the application system which can be separately generated?

- (a) entire systems
- (b) single on-line transaction or batch program
- (c) other (please specify)

8.8 What is the smallest component which can be separately compiled?

8.9 Are the generated programs re-entrant, reusable or single thread only?

8.10 What control does the application developer have over the maximum size of the resultant application load modules?

8B Compiler or Interpreter based Systems

(Do not use this Section if Section 8A has been completed.)

8.1 Is the application specification compiled before use?

8.1.1 If so, what is the smallest component that can be compiled separately?

- (a) entire system
- (b) single on-line transaction or batch application
- (c) other (please specify)

8.2 Is the resultant object code the machine code for the target machine?

8.3 If the application specification is modified, is the application recompiled

(a) automatically at the next program execution?

(b) when directed by the user?

(c) at the completion of the edit of the specification?

(d) other? (please specify)

8.4 If the application specification is not automatically recompiled, how is the compiler invoked?

(a) by using job control

(b) using a command within the specification editor

8.5 If the application is compiled, where is the object code placed and what facilities does the user have to specify where it is placed?

9. Screen Definition

9.1 Is the screen definition processor a component of the application generator, part of the host TP system or an additional purchasable component?

9.2 How are the application's screens defined?

(a) interactively, using a 'paint the screen' technique

(b) by specifying field-names and co-ordinates on preformatted help screens

(c) by specifying field-names and co-ordinates within the application definition

(d) by specifying field-names and co-ordinates in the screen definition language of the host TP system

9.3 If a 'screen-painting' technique is used, can the definition be edited?

9.4 If the screen is defined using field co-ordinates, can the screen be displayed immediately?

9.5 Can one screen definition be used by multiple applications?

9.6 Does the screen definition process include generating source statements in the host TP system's screen definition language and then compiling this definition?

10. Screen formats and facilities

10.1 What terminals are supported?

10.2 Is the logical screen size equivalent to the physical (terminal) screen size? If not, what is the maximum logical screen size?

10.3 Is the user's screen format constrained in any way?

(a) by reserved areas for system or error messages

(b) by other application generator information

(c) other constraints such as fixed/pre-determined format

10.4 Can help screens be programmed?

10.5 Can error screens be programmed?

10.6 Can menu screens be programmed?

10.7 Can the following field attributes be specified?

10.7.1 protected

10.7.2 dark (not visible – used for passwords, etc)

10.7.3 high brightness

10.7.4 reverse video

10.7.5 colour

10.7.6 blinking

10.7.7 light pends

10.7.8 other (please specify)

10.8 Are function keys (Program function or control keys) supported?

11. Report Specification

11.1 Does the application generator include a report specification facility?

11.2 How are report formats specified?

(a) interactively using 'screen-painting' techniques

(b) by specifying field-names and co-ordinates on pre-formatted help screens

(c) by specifying field-names and co-ordinates within the application

(d) by specifying field-names and co-ordinates to a separate report writing package

(e) other (please specify)

11.3 If a 'screen-painting' technique is used, can the definition be edited?

11.4 If the report is defined using field co-ordinates, can the report layout be displayed immediately?

11.5 Can the report specification be used within multiple applications?

12. Report Format and Facilities

12.1 Can report output be directed to the VDU initially during development and then to a printer for production operation?

12.2 What options exist for sorting the data to be reported?

12.2.1 Can ascending or descending key sequences be specified?

12.2.2 What is the maximum number of sort keys that can be specified?

12.2.3 Can ascending and descending sequences be inter-mixed?

12.3 Can break functions be specified? If so, what is the maximum number?

12.4 What facilities exist for totalling and other computation?

12.5 Is it necessary to specify field formats or column headings within the report specification? If not, from where are the defaults obtained?

12.6 Can default field formats or column headings be overriden in specific instances?

12.7 What is the maximum number of reports that can be produced within one application?

12.8 Can a report specification be used within many applications?

13. Query Language Facilities

13.1 Does the product include a query language facility?

13.2 Can individual query language statements be executed interactively?

13.3 Does the query language facility operate with all of the file or database structures supported by the application generator? If not, which are not supported?

13.4 Are queries restricted to single files only?

13.5 Does the user have to know the files in which the data items he requires reside?

13.6 Are queries expressed

(a) using a formatted help screen?

(b) using a relational or set-based language?

(c) other? (please specify)

13.7 Are the records or fields retrieved as a result of executing one query saved and available to be used in further queries?

13.8 Can the data retrieved as a result of executing a retrieval be formatted for presentation using the report-writer facilities?

14. Data File and Database Definition

14.1 Is the database or file definition provided as part of the application specification

(a) explicitly?

(b) implicitly?

(c) not part of the application specification?

14.2 Is the database or file definition used by the application specified in the same language as the database or file description used by the DBMS?

14.3 Can the same file or database specification be used by more than one application?

14.4 If the file or database definition is derived from or contained within the application specification, what facilities exist

14.4.1 for tuning the database structure?

14.4.2 for re-organising the database structure?

14.5 What data formats are supported and what are the restrictions on their size?

14.6 Are named group structures supported?

14.7 Are named repeating group structures supported? If so, what is the maximum level of nesting supported

14.7.1 for use on a screen?

14.7.2 for use in a report?

14.7.3 for storage in a file or database record?

14.8 Input Data Validation

14.8.1 Can the following field input validations be specified within the description of a data item?

(a) field is all numeric

(b) field is all alphabetic characters

(c) field is mandatory

(d) field lies within specified ranges

(e) field exists within specified list of values

(f) field is cross-validated with other fields

(g) other (please specify)

14.8.2 What action occurs if an input field fails one of the validation checks?

14.9 What data output representations can be specified when defining a data item?

14.9.1 default column headings

14.9.2 default size (different from storage size)

14.9.3 edited output representation (please indicate how the output representation is specified)

15. Data File and Database Accessing Facilities

15.1 Is the application generator primarily associated with the vendor's own database system?

15.2 What other files and database systems may be accessed?

15.3 What restrictions are imposed when accessing data?

(a) read only

(b) limits on the structured complexity of the database

(c) database or file features or operations not supported

15.4 Can the generated application access files and databases previously created for conventionally programmed applications? If so, how are data representations not supported by the application generator program converted?

15.5 If the application generator is primarily associated with its own database system, how can the data be realistically processed by conventionally produced applications?

15.6 Logical data views

15.6.1 Is the concept of a logical data view supported?

15.6.2 If the view is not restricted to (part of) a single physical record, how is the navigation of the database structure specified?

16. Application Development and Debugging

16.1 Is application development menu-driven?

16.2 Are help screens available?

16.3 Can applications be developed incrementally using a top-down design philosophy? (ie allowing testing with an incomplete application specification).

16.4 Do facilities exist for linking and displaying screen sequences before writing application code?

16.5 Does the product's application specification editor (or data entry system) include interactive syntax checking?

16.6 Can individual application specification statements be executed on entry? If so, can such a sequence of executed statements be saved to form part of an application specification?

16.7 Does the TP system normally have to be brought down or re-started

16.7.1 to include revised screen formats?

16.7.2 to include new screen formats?

16.7.3 to include revised applications?

16.7.4 to include new applications?

16.8 What facilities (please state whether interactive or not) exist for run-time debugging of

16.8.1 on-line applications?

16.8.2 batch applications?

16.9 What facilities exist for checking the consistency and completeness of the system specification? Which of these facilities are interactive?

17. Recovery

17.1 For on-line systems, is database and TP recovery co-ordinated?

17.2 Does the application generator contain its own terminal/ message handler?

17.2.1 If so, what information is logged automatically for recovery purposes?

(a) all system accesses

(b) all input messages

(c) all successful transactions

(d) all output messages

(e) other (please specify)

17.2.2 Does utility software exist to enable messages to be re-processed?

17.3 Does the application generator support recovery for multi-exchange business transactions? If so, are database updates performed using

(a) DBMS handled delayed update technique?

(b) application generator handled delayed update technique (using the scratch pad area)?

(c) application handled delayed update technique (the application specification saving data within the scratch pad area or other files)?

(d) by locking database records across exchanges?

17.4 Does the application generator contain its own DB handler?

17.4.1 If so, what information is logged automatically for recovery purposes

(a) before images?

(b) after images?

(c) database transactions?

(d) other? (please specify)

17.4.2 What utilities exist to facilitate database recovery?

17.5 For batch applications, is checkpointing or any other such recovery technique supported?

17.6 In the event of a system failure during an on-line application, will the user's terminal be recovered to

(a) the end of the last (completed) exchange?

(b) the start of the dialogue?

(c) the log-on sequence only?

(d) a point determined by the application design? (eg start of business transaction)

18. Recovery during Application Specification

In the event of a failure during application development, what provisions exist to facilitate recovery?

SECTION E - SUPPORT AND EXPERIENCE

1. Support

1.1 What maintenance and support services are available

1.1.1 during installation of the product?

1.1.2 once the product is operational?

1.2 Where and by whom is product support undertaken?

1.3 What procedures are available for reporting problems and what action and priorities are assigned to rectifying faults?

1.4 Are new versions of the product automatically sent to users?

1.5 What is the policy for supporting previous releases of the product and how many versions do you currently support?

1.6 How upward compatible is the product for changes to

1.6.1 the hardware?

1.6.2 the operating system?

1.7 Are there facilities for users to 'customise' the product?

1.8 To what extent is modification by users allowed without affecting support?

2. Documentation

2.1 What manuals and other documentation are provided free of charge when the product is purchased? What is the level of reference for each manual eg management overview, system designer, application programmer, operator, etc?

2.2 What other 'optional' manuals are available?

3. Training

3.1 What training is required in order to operate and use the system? What training is provided free of charge when the product is purchased? What additional training is available?

3.2 Do you provide appropriate training courses on your premises? Can you provide appropriate training on-site?

4. Costs

(When giving prices please indicate whether these are inclusive or exclusive of VAT.)

4.1 How much does it cost to buy the product outright? Does this cost include a copy of the source code?

4.2 How much does it cost to rent or lease the product

4.2.1 per month?

4.2.2 per year?

4.3 What are the minimum and maximum rental periods?

4.4 What are your maintenance terms?

4.5 Can the product be acquired on a trial basis and if so for how long and what are the costs involved? Are these costs discounted from any subsequent purchase price?

4.6 What are your terms for multiple copies of the product

4.6.1 on a single site?

4.6.2 on multiple sites?

4.7 What installation support is included within the purchase price? Does the price include the cost of new versions?

4.8 Is any warranty provided?

4.9 What is the cost of any training not provided free of charge when the product is purchased?

4.10 What is the cost of any manuals not provided free of charge when the product is purchased?

Appendix 3
Application Generator Experiment

BACKGROUND

These are the conclusions of a study into application generators carried out by CCTA (the Central Computer and Telecommunications Agency) of HM Treasury and published as an internal report during 1984.

The experiment was to build a small but non-trivial application system using three representative application generators. The objectives were to compare the different approaches used to specify the application and to gain practical experience in using this important new class of software development tool.

The three generators chosen for the experiment were:

— a product using formatted screens and parameters and involving minimal conventional programming;

— a more conventional programming language incorporating set-based data manipulation concepts;

— a parametric system.

The products used for the experiment are in no way recommended or endorsed or ranked one against the others. One benefit which had not been foreseen was the demonstration facility which it provided. Several departments were given practical demonstrations of the products' capabilities and limitations.

CONCLUSIONS

Each of the three products was capable of producing a system functionally conforming to the design specification (though in one case software problems prevented certain parts from working fully).

The time to produce the system varied from 15 to 25 days. While these systems were not of operational standard, function point analysis suggests that implementing a similar system using conventional techniques would require appreciably more time.

The final systems comprised 1400 to 4800 lines of code. It is estimated that an equivalent COBOL system would require 5000 to 20,000 lines depending on the host database, teleprocessing monitor and operating system.

Each of the products was usable after the short training courses provided by the vendors. Approximately three to four weeks' practical work was necessary to use the products effectively. Expert advice was required from time to time.

While the level of programming skills required varied from almost none to significant, general computer skills were needed for each of the products in order to undertake the technical systems design processes. End-users without computing skills could have used two of the products to interrogate data in existing databases. Corresponding facilities in the other product are also available, but require a second product.

One reason for the high productivity was the ability to amend, compile and test the programs on-line although this encouraged a slightly undisciplined approach to design and debugging. All the products would have benefited from some additional debugging aids.

The products were terminal intensive, requiring a terminal for each active programmer. Hard-copy facilities in the form of a fast printer were also necessary for development work.

When designing systems, advantage should be taken of special facilities included within the intended target software. A general specification (like that used for this experiment) could not always do this.

Where systems are capable of producing structured documentation, advantage should be taken of this.

No accurate measure of the amount of computer time used during the development is available, but indications from one system were that the development load was not substantially greater than normal interactive development. The incremental way in which the systems were developed, without large compilations, was probably resource efficient. No measure of efficiency of the completed systems is available.

Appendix 4
Example of System Development

In order to help those who are new to a study of this area, an outline description is given of the sequence of events which typically takes place during the initial set-up and programming of an application.

The example which follows is extremely simple; this is deliberate in order to illustrate in sufficient clarity various features of application generators. It concerns a company's personnel system, which is also used as the basis of their telephone directory; it produces a printed telephone directory and various other reports and is also used for on-line queries.

It should be assumed that the potential users have agreed that this is the system that they desire and, further, that data analysis has shown that there must be an 'Individuals' file, plus a 'Departments' file holding also the manager's name. The actual phone numbers, of which each person may have more than one, are to be held as a completely separate file. There must also be, somewhere in the system, details of the standing information which is needed to print the telephone list, such as numbers which apply to functions rather than individuals, and various instructions; the latter will be held as part of the report specification.

The first process is to set up the file structures, with their data dictionary entries. It is assumed that this includes details of the validation required and column headings for reports. It is necessary to specify at file or field level who is allowed to access the file. This feature is vitally important in the application being considered, because a personnel system contains sensitive confidential information which must be guarded from unauthorised access.

The next process is to set up the input screens, to be used to insert data onto the various files and to make any subsequent amendments. There can be a number of different mechanisms for this purpose, such as:

- screen painting, where it is possible to start from a blank screen and to build up a picture of the screen as it will look to its eventual user; details of fields from files, input fields and literals can all be included;
- specifying screen co-ordinates; where one builds up a table of entries specifying row, column and content as well as attributes such as screen brightness, colour (where appropriate) and cursor positioning;
- line by line specification of co-ordinates, as above, where in addition the results of each line of entry are displayed on a representation of the screen.

In this example, 'specifying screen co-ordinates' is used. The input screens required include:

- enter new starters;
- amend personnel data;
- delete personnel data;
- add new department;
- amend department;
- delete department;
- add individual's telephone number;
- delete telephone number;
- add telephone number for function.

To use this mode of screen definition, a proforma is used to indicate where information such as the rubric identifying fields and the data to be displayed is to appear on the screen, as shown on the example ('AMEND DEPARTMENT FILE') in Figure A4.1.

The input screens can now be used for two purposes; firstly to show the users what this part of the system will look like while it is

ROW	COL	FIELD NAME or LITERAL	KEY FOR RELATED DATA
1	1	%DATE	
1	25	"AMEND DEPARTMENT DATA"	
4	10	"DEPARTMENT"	
4	23	DEPARTMENT.DEPTCODE	
4	30	DEPARTMENT.DEPTNAME	
8	10	"COST CENTRE"	
8	23	DEPARTMENT.COSTCENTRE	
12	10	"MANAGER"	
12	23	DEPARTMENT.MANAGERCODE	
14	23	PERSONNEL.NAME	DEPARTMENT.MANAGERCODE
17	5	"LAST AMENDED"	
17	23	DEPARTMENT.DATEAMEND	

The resultant screen will appear like this;

```
25 DEC 1986                 AMEND DEPARTMENT DATA

          DEPARTMENT     2000    ACCOUNTS


          COST CENTRE    14-99


          MANAGER        J965

                         Mr F Wizard

     LAST AMENDED        1 JAN 1985
```

Figure A4.1 Amend Department File

still easy to make alterations to suit their needs, and secondly to allow the input of data for testing purposes. Since there is a utility for making simple enquiries (on single records) included in the software package, as is normal, this will be used to check the results of input. This will provide an independent check on the contents of the files after updating.

As soon as the basic reports and queries required by the system (in this case the telephone list and various personnel reports) have been added to the system, which is the next stage, the system will be ready for initial demonstration to its users. Here it may become apparent that changes need to be made; for example, to column headings on reports or, more importantly, to the data reported. It is important to involve end-users in this process to ensure that they like what they see and are able to confirm that the system is providing the service that they require.

The next important stage is to link together all the components into a coherent system. In this case this is done by building up a control structure of hierarchical menus. Further testing will be required of the linked system – to ensure that the whole system still does what the component parts did under test conditions. In devising a test plan it is likely that a more thorough coverage of the testing needed can be provided from data that has been created specially than from more random data transferred from an existing system. The transferred data is likely to be of great help in providing realistic test data for testing the effect of large volumes of data on the system later, when the tests for correctness have been completed.

Finally one must make sure that the system is acceptable to its users. End-user acceptance must be subject to a previously agreed test plan. One can accept minor changes at this stage, and indeed it is believed that this is one of the major benefits of using application generators, but some limit must normally be set since otherwise one can enter a seemingly never-ending loop of changes. This does not of course prevent genuinely evolutionary or incremental development, where one plans to add 'bells and whistles' to the system after it has been in use for a while, or perhaps to fulfil a particularly urgent need in the short term and to add extra facilities later.

This discussion of a simple but typical development is relevant to a study of 'features' because as each stage is examined in more detail various features will stand out as particularly important.

Appendix 5
References and Bibliography

CCTA (Ed Dee), *Application Generation,* IT Series No 3, HMSO, 1983

Chard, R A, *Evaluating Program Generators for Micros,* NCC Publications, 1985

Christoff, K A, 'Building a Fourth Generation Environment', *Datamation,* Vol 31, No 19, pp 118-124, 15 September 1985

Damodaran, L, Simpson, A, Wilson, P A, *Designing Systems for People,* NCC Publications, 1980

Evans, Paul, 'Users Speak Out on 4GLs', *IBM Computer Today,* 6 November 1985

Forage, Geoff, 'Fourth-Generation Languages and Advanced Software Development', *Data Processing,* Vol 27, No 9, pp 6-8, November 1985

Forage, Geoff, *The INBUCON Survey of Fourth Generation Languages,* INBUCON, 1985

Garrett, Alex, 'Emerging Remedies for an Old Headache', *Computing, the Magazine,* pp 16-17, 23 May 1985

Grindley, Kit, 'Something for Everyone – the 1985 Urwick/*Computing* Survey', *Computing, the Magazine,* 4 July 1985

Horowitz, E, Kuyper, A and Narasimilian, B, 'A Survey of Application Generators', *IEEE Software,* pp 40-54, January 1985

Hyldon, Michael, 'Feeling the Effect of a New Life-cycle', *Computing, the Magazine,* 21 March 1985

Grindley, Kit (Ed), *4GLs – A Survey of Best Practice; the Report of the IDPM Working Party,* IDPM, 1986

Nelson, Keith, *4GLs – A Survey of UK Available Products,* CSC and IDPM, 1986

Jenkins, A Milton, 'Surveying the Software Generator Market', *Datamation,* pp 105-120, September 1985

Lobell, R F, *Application Program Generators,* NCC Publications, 1983

Longworth, G, *Designing for Change,* NCC Publications, 1985

Martin, James, *Fourth Generation Languages,* Vols 1 & 2, Savant 1983 and 1984

Martin, James, *Fourth-Generation Languages,* Vol 1 – Principles, Prentice-Hall, 1985

Martin, James, *Fourth-Generation Languages,* Vol 2 – Products, Prentice-Hall, 1986

Mayne, A and Wood, M, *Introducing Relational Database,* NCC Publications, 1984

Morrison, R, '4GLs vs COBOL', *Computerworld,* 12 August 1985

Nelson, Keith, 'Technical Requirements of Fourth Generation Languages', *Data Processing,* Vol 27, No 9, pp 12-15, November 1985

Orr, Ken, 'Managing the Software Crisis', *Computerworld,* 15 & 22 July 1985

Watts, Richard, *Introducing Interactive Computing,* NCC Publications, 1984

Watts, Richard, 'Fourth-Generation Languages – How to Choose the Right One', *Data Processing,* Vol 27, No 9, pp 9-11, November 1985

Whiteside, D and Hughes, N, 'Selection Starts for "True" Fourth Generation', *DEC User,* May 1985

Index